George Junkin

A Treatise on Sanctification

George Junkin

A Treatise on Sanctification

ISBN/EAN: 9783337414870

Printed in Europe, USA, Canada, Australia, Japan

Cover: Foto ©Lupo / pixelio.de

More available books at **www.hansebooks.com**

TREATISE

ON

SANCTIFICATION.

BY
GEORGE JUNKIN, D.D. LL.D.,
LATE PRESIDENT OF WASHINGTON COLLEGE, AT LEXINGTON, VA.

PHILADELPHIA:
PRESBYTERIAN BOARD OF PUBLICATION,
No. 821 Chestnut Street.

CONTENTS.

	PAGE
PREFACE	7

CHAPTER I.
HOLINESS—THE TERM AND THING DEFINED.................. 9

CHAPTER II.
HAPPINESS—SPRINGS FROM LEGITIMATE ACTION.......... 14

CHAPTER III.
HOLINESS AND HAPPINESS—THEIR RELATIONS AND PROPORTIONS... 21

CHAPTER IV.
MAN IS UNHOLY... 25

CHAPTER V.
MAN'S INABILITY TO MAKE HIMSELF HOLY..................... 27

CHAPTER VI.
SANCTIFICATION IS THAT PROCESS BY WHICH HOLINESS IS REPRODUCED IN THE SOULS OF MEN................................. 32

CHAPTER VII.
THE HOLY GHOST, THE SANCTIFIER................................ 44

CONTENTS.

CHAPTER VIII.
ON REGENERATION—SANCTIFICATION BEGUN 49

CHAPTER IX.
THE NECESSITY OF REGENERATION 59

CHAPTER X.
REGENERATION MYSTERIOUS—OBJECTIONS 63

CHAPTER XI.
EVIDENCES OF REGENERATION 70

CHAPTER XII.
THE INHABITATION OF THE SPIRIT 80

CHAPTER XIII.
ON SAVING FAITH 84

CHAPTER XIV.
ON REPENTANCE UNTO LIFE 90

CHAPTER XV.
SANCTIFICATION COMPARED WITH JUSTIFICATION 98

CHAPTER XVI.
THE ORDER OF THE GRACES 102

CHAPTER XVII.
PROGRESSIVE NATURE OF SANCTIFICATION 106

CHAPTER XVIII.
INSTRUMENTALITIES BY WHICH THE SPIRIT WORKS IN THE PROGRESS OF SANCTIFICATION 117

CHAPTER XIX.
TEMPTATION AND PRAYER—MEANS OF GROWTH 126

CHAPTER XX.

THE FRUIT OF THE SPIRIT.. 132

CHAPTER XXI.

SANCTIFICATION IMPERFECT—OBJECTION............................... 137

CHAPTER XXII.

SANCTIFICATION COMPLETED, NEGATIVELY—REMARKS ON IDENTITY.. 141

CHAPTER XXIII.

SANCTIFICATION POSITIVE—RUNS INTO ETERNITY................... 148

CHAPTER XXIV.

THE JUDGMENT—A CONFIRMATION IN BLISS: NOT AN END OF MORAL GOVERNMENT... 156

PREFACE.

THIS little treatise on SANCTIFICATION is designed as a counter-part to my book on JUSTIFICATION. This latter, published first in 1839 took its rise from the agitations of the times, caused by innovations upon our doctrinal standards, which seriously affected that great central doctrine of Christianity. Its substance was first given to the public in the VINDICATION, in 1836: which was used on the appeal before the General Assembly of that year. Inasmuch, however, as that was both controversial and judicial, it appeared to me advisable to strip the matter of that form, and present the doctrines in a shape better adapted for general reading. To the second edition of that work was added a short chapter on Sanctification. That brief appendix is now expanded in this little volume. It is, of course, more practical than the former treatise: that, regards legal relations; this, moral and spiritual qualities. The doctrines, however, of the two books are inseparable from each other, and from practical religion. Without the atonement, no sinner can be pardoned. Without the righteousness—the perfect obedience of Christ, no sinner can be justified. Without pardon and justification no sinner can be sanctified. And without sanctification—holiness, no man shall see the Lord.

The agitations of these times having thrown me out of regular employment, in the pulpit; it occurred to me and to others, that the pen and the press, both rivals and aids to the pulpit, might enable me still to preach the ever-blessed gospel, and that, even after I shall have passed away beyond the agitations of wars and rumours of wars.

The Lord accompany, by his Holy Spirit, both this and its predecessor, so shall my feeble labours become instrumental in saving souls; and to his name be all the glory evermore. Amen.

A TREATISE ON SANCTIFICATION.

CHAPTER I.

HOLINESS—THE TERM AND THING DEFINED.

THE meaning of words in the New Testament, used to express ideas common to it with the Old, cannot be certainly and safely ascertained by reference to classical Greek. As they are virtually translations, we are bound to define and limit them by the meaning of the words, in Old Testament writings, for which they stand. This rule of interpretation is a necessity springing from the imperfection of all human language. Words are not, correctly speaking, *vehicles* of thought, as they are often called: but only arbitrary, conventional instruments for calling up or *suggesting* thoughts, which have previously existed in the mind of the person to whom they are addressed. To one born blind, the words *red, white*, and *blue*, give no ideas, but simply that of sounds; but to him who has had the conception of these colours, the words at once recall them. Moreover, words are very generally inadequate instruments—they fall short of a full and accurate suggestion of ideas. This is felt by all writers and all readers; and often leads to the accumulating of terms—the piling up of epithets, whereby the writer or speaker labours to develop his idea by many words, which he would not do if one could accomplish the object. And yet, after all this accumulation, it is felt that the thought is very imperfectly presented.

We are necessitated, therefore, to look to Old Testament usage in settling the meaning of New Testament words and phrases.

The term Sanctification and its cognates come prominently under this law of hermeneutics. The primary idea, suggested by it, is the setting apart of the object or subject from a common to a special use or service—but generally a religious use. Jeremiah (vi. 4,) calls upon the children of Benjamin to sanctify war against Jerusalem—"*prepare* ye war against her." Israel was commanded to sanctify all the first born. Thus the seventh day was sanctified—set apart to the special use of mental, moral, and religious culture: the materials for the construction of the tabernacle were dedicated—consecrated to this particular religious use. So the Israelitish people —so all who are admitted by baptism into the visible church are holy unto the Lord. See Exod. iii. 5: xvi. 23: xix. 6: xx. 8: Matt. vii. 6: 1 Cor. iii. 17: 2 Pet. i. 18.

But the secondary and most common use, at least in the New Testament, is that of preparation for sacred service. This comes within the region of morals. The term *sanctification*, literally means the process of making holy; and implies a deficiency or absence of the qualities expressed by the word holy. *Holiness* is an abstract term, expressive of the entire sum of moral perfections. The inscription on the high priest's mitre—" Holiness to the Lord,"—is an ascription to him of all moral excellence: "Who is like unto thee, glorious in *holiness.*" " God sitteth upon the throne of his *holiness.*" " Once I have sworn by my *holiness.*" "Judah hath profaned the *holiness* of the Lord." In this absolute sense the term is not applied to imperfect beings: yet may we speak of the thing, and so also explain the term—under the two-fold distinction, of freedom from all impurity, sin, imperfection, on the one hand; and of the possession of all purity, uprightness, and perfection, on the other. And for convenience we shall designate these two aspects, by the epithets *negative holiness,* and *positive holiness.*

Negative holiness is ascribable to God; to the angels, who have kept their integrity and consequently their first estate, and to the spirits of just men made perfect; but not to men upon earth and yet compassed with infirmity.

" I find no fault in him," is the testimony of the miserable judge who delivered over the Holy

One of Israel to the executioners, and "there is *no iniquity* with the Lord our God." "He is the rock, his work is perfect; for all his ways are judgment; a God of truth and *without iniquity*, just and right is he." "Shall not the judge of all the earth do right?" But in this negative sense *sanctification* cannot be spoken of God while holiness may; he cannot be *made* holy, for there is no impurity to be removed. Yet we are commanded, "Sanctify the Lord of hosts himself—" (Isa. viii. 13,) and it is foretold "They shall sanctify my name, and sanctify the Holy One of Jacob, and shall fear the God of Israel." (Isa. xxix. 23.) But here the primary sense of the word is to be understood,—they shall consecrate—set apart God, in the temple of their hearts and hold him only as the object of their supreme love and adoration.

Neither can the angels be negatively sanctified. They have no corruption to be removed, and are in this negative sense holy already. But positively they are capable of sanctification by an increase of purity and perfection, as we shall see.

The same is true of redeemed spirits already in heaven. They are perfectly holy by negation; yet will they be sanctified in the other sense, by perpetual increase in spiritual excellence. But whilst here in the flesh, even in the negative sense, holiness cannot be ascribed to men, but very partially; and sanctification, in both senses, is expressive of their condition who believe in the Saviour of lost men: the process is advancing, but not complete.

Holiness, viewed as a positive state, is the possession of moral qualities, and the presence of these entitles the person to the epithet *holy*. "The Lord hath sworn by his holiness." (Amos iv. 2.) "Without holiness no man shall see the Lord." (Heb. xii. 14.) The former passage pledged the entire attributes of Jehovah for the punishment of Israel's sin; and when he confirmed the gospel promise by an oath, he pledged all his divine perfections for the security of his redeemed. In this sense all those passages are to be understood which ascribe holiness to the Lord: "Give thanks at the remembrance of his holiness—" "Judah hath profaned the holiness of the Lord." And so, the seraphic doxology, "Holy, Holy, Holy is the Lord God Almighty"— ascribes to him all good and excellent and glorious attributes—justice and mercy, goodness and truth. "God is a Spirit, infinite, eternal, and unchangeable, in his being, wisdom, power, holiness, justice, goodness and truth;" and the summation of all these we have in that one divine word—*God is Love*.

CHAPTER II.

HAPPINESS—SPRINGS FROM LEGITIMATE ACTION.

"HAPPY are thy men," said the queen of Sheba, after witnessing the elegancies of the royal palace, the richness and splendour of its decorations, the number, dress, and beautiful order of his retinue, as it was established under the direction and by the taste of the most learned and scientific of Israel's kings. "*Happy* are thy men, *happy* are these thy servants, which stand continually before thee, and that hear thy wisdom." (1 Kings, x. 8.) "Whoso trusteth in the Lord, *happy* is he."—"He that keepeth the law is *Happy.*"—"*Happy* is that people whose God is the Lord."—"*Happy* is the man that findeth wisdom."—"*Happy* is the man whom God correcteth."—"*Happy* is he which hath mercy on the poor." From such statements it is obvious that happiness is found in a great variety of circumstances, and springs from a great variety of relations: and it is an interesting inquiry, what is that, which, being common to all, justifies the common appellation, *happy*, as applied to all?

Is it not this? that in all these circumstances

and relations, there are called into action some right principles or powers of our nature; and that they are legitimately and duly exercised. If this be so, then we might define happiness by its origin and cause; and say it is a state of mind resulting from the legitimate activity of our faculties of body, mind, and heart. Johnson's definition—"Happiness is the multiplication of agreeable consciousness," would require the latter phrase—*agreeable consciousness*—to be itself defined. But what we here propose coincides with the facts of these and innumerable other cases.

1. There is always *activity* of body, mind, or heart, wherever we use the word *happy*, as descriptive of our feelings. When we look upon a beautiful flower, painting, statue, articles of furniture; or listen to a piece of well-composed and well-executed music, our material frame is called into a state of high excitement, of thrilling action, and we are pleased, delighted, happy. Some of these may moreover affect more than the bodily organs.

A painting may, whilst it thrills the nerves, also, by its historic substance, at once call the understanding and even the reason and moral affections into active play. "The crossing of the Alps," or, "the crossing of the Delaware;" "the embarking of the Pilgrims:" "the star spangled banner," or, "rally round the flag, boys;" what conceptions in the understanding and what overwhelming passions do they not arouse? Let any man look within his own bosom, and he will perceive not only the blood coursing his veins more rapidly, and his nerves quivering throughout his whole system; but his intellect grasping magnificent thoughts: and his moral sympathies bearing onward in the most intense activity. Now these activities place the mind in that state called *happy*, and this happiness is characterized by its antecedent cause. Each peculiar form of action has its own peculiar emotion. If the excitation lies in the bodily organs only, it will be followed by a state of mind which we should denominate *pleasure*. The lowest of these forms of happiness which result from the gratification of the mere animal appetites, are, to a large degree, common to us with the mere animals. And when men are content with these, or look to them as their chief good, they are exceedingly likely to make them their god and to give them illicit adoration—" Whose god is their belly and whose glory is their shame."

2. Hence the limitation of activities, in our definitions, to those which are *legitimate*. Fully aware of the tendency to excess and the deception practised by calling corrupt pleasures by the name of happiness, we would guard against it. Malachi reproves Israel—" We call the proud happy; yea, they that work wickedness are even set up." This misapplication is often mischievous; for, when all accounts are balanced, unlawful actions do not find

the balance on the credit side of the sheet. "Remember that thou in thy lifetime receivedst thy good things, and likewise Lazarus evil things: but now he is comforted, and thou art tormented." Whatever is in excess beyond legitimate use of God's good creatures, will recoil. No man can violate the laws of God, physical, intellectual, or moral, with impunity. If he eat and drink to excess, he may deceive himself into the belief that his pleasures are happiness, but misery will follow, and gout may throw the balance against him. Happiness, after all, is as the gratification of legitimate desire.

3. There is a phrase in which our topic has to do with the idea of a negation. As happiness implies a positive activity, the negation of action implies the absence of enjoyment, but not a contradictory state—not a condition of misery. The clod and the stone are not happy, neither are they miserable. But, it may occur, does not the removal of pain—its mere absence, bring pleasure? Doubtless felicity, less or more, is always experienced on such occasions. It is not however a mere negation, when the aching wound, either in the flesh literally, or in the spirit, is healed. It is the absence of positive activity, contrary to the laws of body and mind: and it is the return of either or both to their state of legitimate activity which is the cause of the pleasure. The removal of an evil, which is an unnatural state of the system, in viola-

tion of its laws, is necessarily and instantaneously followed by the restoration of its proper functions, in other words, of its legitimate activities.

4. Or, to give another turn to the thought—it is the unvarying activity of the supreme law of life, self-love that secures happiness. This law is universal as living existence. Every living thing, I was about to say; every living thing desires its own happiness. We imply as much when we indulge the poetic formula—"The earth mourneth and languisheth," "the earth mourneth and fadeth away," "the new wine mourneth, the vine languisheth." Thus sacred poetry represents the love of life of the vegetable fighting for its own well-being. And it also represents the young ravens as crying unto God, and all the beasts of the field looking, and not in vain, unto him for their food. "The young lions roar after their prey, and seek their meat from God." (Ps. civ. 21.) But this is poetry. Very true; and poetry is more natural than prose; and it is more easily understood. There is a love of life in the young dahlias, and the young lilies, which God clothes so beautifully: and in the young lions, whom he feeds in the desert.

5. But this law of life is found, of course, in a higher development, in the higher nature. It is as necessary within the sphere of morals and religion as it is among the lilies of the field, the prowling inhabitants of the desert, the tenants of the air, and the monsters of the deep. Insects and

creeping things; birds and beasts; men, angels, and devils;—all, all are subjects of this first law of nature—self-love—a prime necessity to self-preservation.

Without this, moral government is impossible—inconceivable. For, if the desire of happiness, the love of life were not, then pain and pleasure were as impossible to a man as to a mushroom; to an angel of glory, as to a cedar of Lebanon; to a demon in the bottomless pit, as to a rock in the profound of Vesuvius. But now, if the bruising of my flesh or the wounding of my immortal part, were a matter of entire indifference—if I were insensible to pain or to happiness, how could you address motive to me? How could I be influenced by hope or by fear? How could promises to obedience or threatenings to disobedience be of any avail? But, take away the ideas of reward and of punishment, and what have you left of moral government? "If the foundations be destroyed what can the righteous do?" (Ps. xi. 3.)

Of approach toward this fearful precipice, there are some alarming symptoms in our country. Our free suffrage—the very expression, "the will of the people is the law of the land," generates—or at least hath a strong tendency in the carnal mind, to generate the idea, that the will of man, within the sphere of law, politics, and trade, has superseded the will of God: and it is greatly to be feared, we have millions of population, in whom this freedom of will has already run out into the grossest infidelity; yea into blank, bold, and soul-destroying atheism. Certainly, subjection to the will of God as such; whether made known in his word, or by the glimmering lights of unsanctified reason, have little practical influence in ruling the understandings, swaying the hearts, and regulating the conduct of that large population which flood us from the overflowings of the Danube and the Elbe, the Scheldt, the Mayne and the Rhine.

CHAPTER III.

HOLINESS AND HAPPINESS—THEIR RELATIONS AND PROPORTIONS.

The reader is doubtless prepared to fall in with our first position in this chapter; viz. That holiness, in the order of nature, precedes happiness: that a holy being, in the sense explained, must necessarily be happy; and an unholy one must, by a like necessity, be unhappy. This seems to be an unavoidable deduction from the preceding discussions. Assuming that God is holy and just, exercising over all his works a government like himself, it is impossible not to see that the protection and defence of those who do no iniquity, but keep the commandments of God, must constitute a large part of his actual rule; and the punishment of all iniquity its counterpart. And such is the testimony of holy Scripture. "God is angry with the wicked every day;" "he loveth righteousness and judgment." In Heb. xii. 14, we are commanded to "follow peace with all men, and holiness, without which no man shall see the Lord." So Matt. v. 8, "Blessed are the pure in heart, for they shall see God." Now for our purpose, whether the beatific vision is mainly here intended or not, these are pointed proofs of the necessity of holiness, in order to happiness. There are two words translated *blessed* in the New Testament. One of these signifies a benediction, simply calling for good words upon the person—as Luke xix. 38, "Blessed—be the king—let the king be well spoken of, who cometh in the name of the Lord." (Eph. i. 3,) "Blessed—well spoken of—be the Father of our Lord, &c." The other word which occurs in the eight beatitudes, one of which has just been quoted, signifies, *happy*, and that is here used in a simply declarative sense, not in the form of a benediction or supplication of a good. He does not say, let them be blessed—let a blessing come upon them, but asserts the fact: "Happy are the pure in heart, for they shall see God." In this and Heb. xii. 14, the connection between holiness and happiness is very distinctly affirmed, and I think their relative position too. The order of time in regard to graces we cannot be said to define; but at least there is an order of nature, in which we can speak with safety of them. As truth is in order to goodness, so holiness is in order to happiness; holiness is uniform and necessary antecedent; and happiness is uniform and necessary consequent; that is, one is cause, the other is effect.

The same appears from 1 John iii. 2, 3; "Beloved, now are we the sons—begotten ones of God, and it doth not yet appear what we shall be, but we know that, when he shall appear, we shall be like him; for we shall see him as he is. And every one that hath this hope in him purifieth himself even as he is pure." Now, as will appear hereafter, regeneration is the beginning of sanctification, and as the word *sons* is equivalent to begotten ones—regenerated ones, the apostle makes this the starting point of our transformation into his likeness: and by consequence our introduction to the beatific vision. Purification thus runs parallel with happiness. So in Ps. xxiv. 3-5. "Who shall ascend into the hill of the Lord? or who shall stand in his holy place? He that hath clean hands, and a pure heart; who hath not lifted up his soul unto vanity, nor sworn deceitfully. He shall receive the blessing from the Lord, and righteousness from the God of his salvation." Here again the glory and felicity of heaven are consequent upon holiness—clean hands and a pure heart.

The beatific vision is that direct and immediate vision, contemplation, beholding of God in the heavenly world, of which we can have but feeble conception. "It doth not yet appear what we shall be, but we * * * shall be like him, for we shall see him as he is." "Now we see through a glass darkly, then face to face." No man, John tells us, hath seen God at any time; that is, the pure Godhead apart from the humanity. But these passages, and Job xix. 26, where he assures us that, "in my flesh shall I see God," do surely set forth a vision yet future—a vision or beholding of God in the world of glory, transcending all possible conceptions of the human mind, while here in the flesh. And what is specially pertinent to our purpose, this beatific vision is consequent upon holiness, and without this no man shall enjoy it.

Now if holiness is so indispensable and so efficient, we may fairly conclude that all advances in holiness will run parallel with happiness. In other words, that purity of heart is not only the necessary antecedent, but also the measure of bliss. This, however, we must postpone until we come to treat of the progressive nature of sanctification.

CHAPTER IV.

MAN IS UNHOLY.

No person can cast his eye over the world in which we dwell, without discovering evidence of fearful depravity. Our history is one continued narrative of folly, vice, and wickedness. If the countless volumes of this vast criminal record were removed from all our libraries, our literature would be almost annihilated; dislocated fragments only would remain. What have governments been but systems of agencies for practising wickedness? What have kings and princes been but scourges of the nations? And still, after all that God has done toward ameliorating the human condition, "Man's inhumanity to man, makes countless thousands mourn." At no period in our history have there been more horrible exhibitions of human depravity than during these few years past. Heaven-daring impiety vies with man-slaughtering ferocity in filling up the record of man's shame, and treasuring up wrath against the day of wrath, and revelation of the righteous judgments of God.

To this unblushing human record answers, with soul-sickening exactness, the divine testimony.

From the blood of righteous Abel down to the martyrs of early Christianity, blood stains the annals of our race. God came down and inspected the vast area, and behold it was utterly depraved. "And God saw that the wickedness of man was great in the earth, and that every imagination of the thoughts of his heart was only evil continually." "What is man, that he should be clean, and he that is born of a woman that he should be righteous? Behold, he putteth no trust in his saints; yea, the heavens are not clean in his sight. How much more abominable and filthy is man, which drinketh iniquity like water?" (Job xv. 14–16.) And in Rom. iii., the apostle sums up a series of texts in proof of the doctrine of total depravity. "As it is written, There is none righteous, no, not one. There is none that understandeth, there is none that seeketh after God. They are all gone out of the way, they are together become unprofitable; there is none that doeth good, no, not one. Their throat is an open sepulchre; with their tongues they have used deceit; the poison of asps is under their lips: whose mouth is full of cursing and bitterness: their feet are swift to shed blood: destruction and misery are in their ways: and the way of peace have they not known: there is no fear of God before their eyes." But it is unnecessary to dwell on this point. In theory, all men admit this total depravity, and in practice they demonstrate it. The evidence is complete.

CHAPTER V.

MAN'S INABILITY TO MAKE HIMSELF HOLY.

The man who violates law comes under its curse, and pollutes and disables himself from all holy actions. The fountain is corrupted, and "who can bring a clean thing out of an unclean?" "Not one," is Job's answer. Adam, that is man, by his sin lost " that righteousness wherein he was created; incurred the corruption of his nature, whereby he is utterly indisposed, disabled, and made opposite to all that is spiritually good, and wholly inclined to all evil, and that continually :"—(*Confession*, p. 153.) " Man, by his fall into a state of sin, hath wholly lost all ability of will to any spiritual good accompanying salvation: so as a natural man being altogether averse from that which is good, and dead in sin, is not able, by his own strength, to convert himself, or to prepare himself thereto." (*Confession*, p. 47.) So the Scriptures teach. " For when we were yet *without strength*, in due time Christ died for the ungodly." (Rom. v. 6.) " Because the carnal mind is enmity against God; for it is not subject to the law of God, neither indeed can be." (Rom. viii. 7.) "For without me, ye can do nothing." (John xv. 5.) "Therefore said I unto you, that no man can (δύναται, is able) come unto me, except it were given unto him of my Father." (John vi. 45, 65.)

Now " a rational agent is said to be able to do a given thing, when, upon the putting forth of his energies toward that thing, it is done : and when it does not follow upon such exertion of his powers, he is said *to be unable*. In other words, *ability* implies the existence of a power of causation, and always refers to the proper effect. Every effect is proportioned to its cause, both in nature or quality, and in degree. Like produces like. Physical ability can produce only physical results. Strength, or mere brutal force, can affect only strength or resistance of the same kind. Intellectual ability can be efficient only to intellectual results. Intellectual power or ability may plan the machinery whereby a man can lift a ton weight : but to say that a man's intellect has ability to lift a ton, is absurd, equally with affirming that mere natural strength is able to plan the machinery. Nor is the absurdity a whit less, when it is affirmed that man has natural ability to perform a moral act. Each part of his nature—his animal, his intellectual, his moral powers—has its own peculiar ability—one faculty or class of faculties cannot perform the functions of another. Animal ability (or strength) and intellectual or moral results: intellectual ability and animal or moral results; and moral ability, and intellectual or animal results, are all equally absurd. To yield obedience is a moral result—to repent (I mean saving repentance) is a moral operation—to believe in and love God, are not animal, nor intellectual, nor physical effects or results, but moral; yea, the very essence of all morality, and therefore, in the very nature of the thing, no natural ability of any conceivable kind can qualify man to repent and love God. Moral ability alone can qualify him—by that only can he turn to God and live in him. Now this moral ability exists not in the soul unborn of the Spirit. There death reigns until the Spirit of life takes up his abode there." *Vindication*, pp. 51, 52.

Sec. 2. This utter inability is itself a sin; and this corruption and carnality and enmity are not self-apologetic: they do not excuse the perpetrators, do not release them from obligations to law, and to love and serve God with a pure heart fervently. If it were otherwise—if sin were its own excuse— if the gambling spendthrift could cancel his bond with an empty purse: why then commerce would stagnate, because credit would die. Let a man's wicked moral bankruptcy be recognised as a foreclosure of all demands of duty; and social order and Christian morality are gone. Satan and his followers are at once independent of the moral government of the universe. Against such consequences, however, the Bible and sound reason, which never are opposed, completely protect us; inasmuch as they hold men to their accountability, notwithstanding their spiritual bankruptcy.

Were it not so, no moral agent could commit more than one sin: for being then corrupted and disabled, and made opposite to all good, he cannot, according to this theory, be held accountable any farther: no law extends over him. But sin is not imputed where there is no law. John tells us that "sin is the transgression of the law," (1 John iii. 4,) and Paul says, "Where there is no law, there is no transgression." But Satan and his associates are not the only free intelligences of the universe, as this theory teaches. They are just as much bound by Divine authority as the angels in glory and the spirits of just men made perfect. Their secession does not place them outside and beyond the range of Jehovah's empire. "Wash ye, make you clean" —"O Jerusalem, wash thine heart from wickedness"—"Turn ye, turn ye from your evil ways." All commands to sinners to forsake their sins are declarations of their legal and rightful obligations to Divine authority. "Draw nigh to God, and he will draw nigh to you: cleanse your hands, ye sinners, and purify your hearts, ye double minded." (Jas. iv. 8.) *Repent, believe.* All such are commandments of authority, and are binding wherever applicable. Angels of glory and devils in hell; souls redeemed and in heaven; and souls lost and in the burning lake, are as really and as truly subject to the government of God, as are saints and sinners in this middle region where we dwell. Indeed, we challenge the human intellect to conceive of an intelligent being, endowed with a moral sense, that is under no obligation to submit to its Creator's authority.

CHAPTER VI.

SANCTIFICATION IS THAT PROCESS BY WHICH HOLINESS IS RE-PRODUCED IN THE SOULS OF MEN—ITS INSTRUMENTALITIES.

THE word *process* is here used, for the purpose of expressing the idea of complexity. This is not an *act*, accomplished in an instant, but a *work*, consisting of a variety of operations; and implies a variety of instrumentalities and agencies, and these operating in diversities of methods, times, and seasons. As a work we may analyze it into its *instrumentalities* or the instruments employed in and about the operations; and its *efficient agent*—the Divine Spirit, by whose life-giving power the whole change is effected.

In this chapter let us take up the *Instrumentalities*.

. 1. And first, in general we may say, that the entire arrangements and doings of Divine providence in reference to each individual whom the Lord will bring unto glory, are parts and portions of his instruments for their sanctification. Known unto God are all his works; he governs all his creatures and all their actions; and it is because he foreordains whatsoever comes to pass, that he knows them all. Of this infinite series of events, all that precede regeneration are preparatory instruments.

2. The place of one's birth has much to do with these preparatory steps. Birth in a Christian land; and especially of Christian parents, is ordered of God, with direct reference to the great purposes of his mercy. Compare your condition, reader, in these regards, with that of the Japanese, the Chinese, the Hindoo, the Persian, the wild Arab of the desert, the youth of Timbuctoo, the Red man of our wilderness, the citizens of Naples, old Rome, or southern Ireland; and how obviously is God's partiality to you displayed? Why are you thus favoured? Is it not that you may have access to all the means of grace, and may thus early be led on in the way to glory? The Lord has thus ensured to you all the other means which he ordinarily uses toward the process of sanctification; and among these, the parental care and solicitude, so indispensable to the very continuance of your being in this world, and in which you have been so distinguished from the great masses of infant humanity. This providence gives you early instruction in the way of salvation. Ere you could be taught the art of reading, you were taught the grand elements of saving doctrine, then, ability to read and opportunity to exert it in searching the

oracles of God, was superinduced; you were led to the open fountains of spiritual knowledge. From the mother's lap and the father's knee, you were carried to the house of God, and there, from the pulpit, the Sabbath-school, and catechetical class, learned the duties and the privileges of religious worship. These invaluable blessings were yours at a period that lies beyond the reach of present reminiscence. Not by memory, but by faith in the testimony of others, you know that God was thus kind and provident.

3. Special providences innumerable lead in the same direction: health and sickness, but in different ways, have conduced to the same end. The former, which ought to be the more influential, has not always, indeed not generally, been so. We often underrate blessings, until they depart. Sickness and pain, evils in themselves, are often used as means for good. The rod and reproof bring wisdom. When we pass down into the valley of the shadow of death—into deep and sore afflictions, we reap the peaceable fruits of righteousness; *i. e.* all reap, who are rightly exercised thereby.

Among these wonder-working providences, none are more conspicuous than *war*. By it, God chastises his church and its members; and makes its fearful burdens instrumental in forcing the attention of sinners and saints to eternal things. In what innumerable instances has the Lord come down recently to the battle-field and the hospital;

and, by occasion of their unutterable sorrows, drawn away the hearts of sinful men toward heavenly things? Oh! what heart-piercing shrieks have gone up, God be merciful to me, a sinner! yea, burst forth, with an earnestness utterly unknown during health and outward prosperity. As the thunder from the watery cloud above him, awaked and aroused the soul of the monk of Eisleben, and led him on toward his conversion; so the thunders of the sulphurous canopy have, by the same Divine energy, made the souls of thousands to feel themselves trembling on the verge of eternity, and constrained them to cry out in painful consternation—oh! what must I do to be saved?

But you will say, it was not the lightning's flash and the thunder's roar that sanctified the soul of Luther, nor was it the miles of blazing lines, nor the long reverberations of the cannon's dread utterances, that could convert the thousands who have ascended from the battle-fields, or returned, maimed in body, but healed in spirit, to the homes of the sorrowful yet rejoicing.

No; but we are speaking of instrumental, not of efficient agencies; and beyond doubt, God has made the wrath of man, in these most fearful developments of it, to praise him, it is devoutly hoped, and he will yet more illustriously display his gracious power amid these awful scenes, and bring the nation down in the dust of humility before the majesty of his own throne.

4. To the ministry of the word we have just alluded, and now allude to the visible ordinances, including the very organization of the church itself, as means both of grace and of growth in grace. On these, however, we may not delay. Let us pay a more marked attention to the truth of the word, the great doctrinal substance, as an instrument. Our Lord, in his prayer, properly called his, says, "Sanctify them through thy truth: thy word is truth."—And "for their sakes, I sanctify myself, that they also might be sanctified through the truth." (John xvii. 17, 19.) So he had before expressed the same (xv. 3.) "Now ye are clean through the word which I have spoken unto you." And Paul says (Eph. v. 26.) "That he might sanctify and cleanse it with the washing of water by the word." James also teaches the instrumentality of the truth, (i. 18): "Of his own will begat he us with the word of truth."

5. The relations of the truth to this great work of sanctification are not so generally agreed upon, among even evangelical men, as could be desired. Has the word of truth an instrumental agency only? or has it an efficient force—a generating power? To the former we return an affirmative and to the latter, a negative response. We believe the Scriptures and the truths they contain, ascribe all efficient agency in the premises to the Holy Spirit: and that the word of truth becomes an efficient instrumentality only when the Spirit employs it.

just so is it with the living ministry: we are mighty to pull down the strongholds of sin and Satan; but it is only "through God." "Our sufficiency is of God." We are commanded to take "the sword of the Spirit, which is the word of God"—(Eph. vi. 17.). Now a sword has in it no power—no efficiency for good or evil. It is perfectly harmless in itself, and will destroy no life and maim no limb. But the sinewy arm that wields it may produce fearful havoc. The analogy is striking. The word of truth—the doctrines of Scripture have no life in themselves, and cannot communicate what they have not. They have an adaptation for use, by a living agent, and whenever the Holy Spirit takes up his sword, it becomes a sharp two-edged instrument, driven home by his almighty hand. All the above and many other scriptures teach the simple instrumentality of the word directly and indirectly: the former on their face and the latter indirectly by imputing the entire life-giving efficacy to the Spirit. Others we may add—"That which is born of the flesh is flesh, and that which is born of the Spirit is spirit." And (John vi. 63,) "It is the Spirit that quickeneth" —*i. e.* that giveth life—and 1 Pet. iii. 18—"Put to death in the flesh, but quickened by the Spirit." Then we may go back to the beginning, and there we find it was the Spirit that generated life from the chaotic mass and that breathed into Adam's nostrils the breath of life—of lives, viz: of the body and the soul. Accordingly, when spiritual life was lost in the transgression, it became, under the new covenant in the economy of redemption, the work of the same Spirit to reproduce this life in the soul; and this is the beginning of sanctification. And 1 Cor. vi. 11, declares, "But ye are washed, but ye are sanctified, but ye are justified in the name of the Lord, and by the Spirit of our God."

But we may not press this farther at present. If the Holy Ghost is the producer and cherisher of life in the soul, as we must see more fully at another time, then it follows, that there is no life-giving power in the truth itself; the letter killeth, it is the Spirit that giveth life; and this presents another part of the process, which is merely preparatory.

6. The relative position of conviction; its nature and agency, and its end.

1. Its *nature and agency*. It is an operation of the understanding—a result of the judging power. When a jury brings in a verdict of guilty, the man is said to be convicted; and the method, by which they reach this result, is the same as any other judgment of the mind. They compare the conduct of the man, as exhibited in the evidence, with the rule as laid down in the law: if the conduct agrees with the law, they so declare, and the man is acquitted. But if they perceive his conduct to coincide with the definition of murder, as contained in the law, they declare the fact so to be; and the

man is convicted. Now, so it is at the bar of conscience. The truths of the moral law are laid along-side of a man's own conduct, as revealed in his consciousness and memory; he compares them together; he perceives their inconsistency, and his conscience pronounces the verdict. So the accusers of the dissolute woman " being convicted by their own conscience, went out."

Such is the province of natural conscience— "Their conscience also bearing witness, and their thoughts the meanwhile accusing or else excusing one another." (Rom. ii. 15.) In the original state of man, this power of conscience was full and adequate. But sin blinded the mind, and conscience is no longer adequate. Its knowledge of the law is too imperfect. The whole mind is so debased and enfeebled, that it is unable to comprehend spiritual things. " But the natural man receiveth not the things of the Spirit of God, for they are foolishness unto him: neither can he know them— (he is not able, οὐ δύναται) because they are spiritually discerned: but he that is spiritual judgeth all things"—(1 Cor. ii. 14.) Hence the inability of conscience to produce thorough conviction of sin: and here it is that the Holy Spirit interposes. He takes up his sword—the doctrines of truth contained in the law, and cuts to the heart—enlightens the mind; quickens the conscience, and leads on to the condition which cries out, " Men and brethren, what must we do?" " O Ephraim, what shall I do unto thee? O Judah, what shall I do unto thee? for your goodness is as a morning cloud, and as the early dew it goeth away. Therefore have I hewed them by the prophets; I have slain them by the words of my mouth: and thy judgments are as the light that goeth forth." (Hos. vi. 4, 5.) Conviction of sin results from the illumination of the mind in the knowledge of the law, and its results are painful, but in various degrees. If depravity has been excessive, and habits of sinning long indulged in, and so deeply rooted; and if the illumination is full and large, the soul must be thrown into great depths of distress—" Out of the depths have I cried unto thee, O Lord."

3. Its *end;* if this is not followed up by a corresponding enlightenment in the truths of the gospel, the painful emotions must be great, and will continue and increase without end. For this anguish there can be found only one remedy—the light beaming from the Sun of righteousness. Hence we remark again,

Conviction of sin, *per se,* is not a blessing. To show me how vile I am, is no favour; unless you show me also how I can escape from my sins and their just consequences. But if the wound in the spirit is speedily followed by the healing balm, then may I desire the stroke of the Divine hand for the sake of what is to follow. I can afford to take the nauseous medicine for its remote sequence: remove this sequence, and I reject the potion.

What is hell but the land of everlasting regrets. "Tophet is ordained of old; yea, for the king it is prepared; he hath made it deep and large; the pile thereof is fire and much wood; and the breath of the Lord, like a stream of brimstone, doth kindle it." (Isa. xxx. 33.)

> "The breath of God, his angry breath,
> Supplies and fans the fire;
> Then sinners taste the second death,
> And would, but can't expire."

But I said the degrees of this conviction, and its painful accompaniments, are vastly various: they indeed range from the dreadful extreme, presented here by the poet, to the slightest painful apprehension, vanishing away into incipient comfort and consolation. For, in the essential nature of conviction, it lies within the region of the intellect, and is clearly distinguishable from the emotional states of the mind—the feelings that accompany it. These views force upon us the inferences.

1. That conviction is not conversion. Many experience clear convictions of sin—they see plainly that they have violated the law and are justly exposed to its penal sanction, who yet go no farther; and stopping short, like the seed by the way-side or on the stony ground, never attain to true conversion. And not a few are thus ruined by falling into the error pointed out in our next inference; viz:

2. That the sorrows which often accompany or follow even defective conviction are mistaken for repentance. Whereas the emotions which accompany the turning of the soul from sin to God, are clearly distinguishable from the turning itself, which is the true idea of repentance, as we shall see anon.

3. A third inference, is the important practical rule—never pray for severe law work upon the conscience. It is not a necessary accompaniment of true conversion. We are not informed that any of the apostles experienced it, except Saul, who was born out of due time. And, though they were pricked in the heart at the pentecostal revival, yet it would seem that their painful emotions were of short duration, and speedily followed by spiritual comfort and good hope through grace. No, the Spirit of all grace can produce the necessary degree of conviction, preparatory to the beginning of actual sanctification, without filling the soul with dreadful terrors and driving it upon the confines of the burning lake. In the regular and orderly state of the church; where the youthful mind is early and earnestly imbued with the precious truths of the word—both of law and gospel—we shall hardly find out the day of our children's conversion, and we and they must learn it by the fruits.

To all these, let us add the power of persuasion—warnings, threatenings, promises, entreaties—all arguments addressed to fear or to hope. "Almost, thou persuadest me to be a Christian." "Knowing the terror of the Lord, we persuade men." Undoubtedly the church, and especially through her ministry, has done much in this line toward the sanctification of lost and polluted man. She is ever ransacking the highways and the hedges and exerting herself to the utmost, compelling them to come in and fill the Lord's house and feast off its fat things. All that is powerful in reasoning; all that is alarming in the terrors of eternal wrath; all that is enticing and attractive in the glories of heavenly felicity; the people of God—the ministry of the word have pressed and do still press upon the consideration of sinners; and this to the utter exhaustion of moral suasion. But all these fall short of that efficiency which brings men into a state of holiness before God. They do not convert the soul. They are only instrumental and preparatory: another power is needed: a real efficient agent having in himself life and holiness, and therefore a capability to generate them in the souls of lost men.

4 *

CHAPTER VII.

THE HOLY SPIRIT THE SANCTIFIER.

That holiness proceeds from the Spirit may well be inferred from the name so frequently given to him in Scripture. David, deploring his own sin and pollution, entreats, "Cast me not away from thy presence, and take not thy Holy Spirit from me." (Ps. li. 11.) In the history of the miraculous conception, he is constantly called the Holy Ghost. Eighty-six times is this appellation given to him in the New Testament, besides four times it is translated Holy Spirit; making ninety times. And all gracious works are ascribed to him. Under the baptism by the Holy Ghost all graces are comprehended. We are baptized in his name equally with that of the Father and of the Son. Because of his work in the miraculous conception, Christ is called the Son of God. "The Holy Ghost shall come upon thee, and the power of the Highest shall overshadow thee: therefore also that holy thing which shall be born of thee, shall be called the Son of God." (Luke i. 35.) Thus, the humanity of the God-man was consecrated, set apart, sanctified by the Spirit; much more, we infer, does the humanity of his redeemed require this sanctification. So the Spirit came upon him at his baptism; at once a significant sign and type of our baptismal consecration to holy service, and of our purification and preparation for it.

But not only by his name and offices just mentioned is his dignity and sanctifying power intimated. The unpardonable nature of the sin against the Holy Ghost establishes the same. "Wherefore I say unto you, all manner of sin and blasphemy shall be forgiven unto men; but the blasphemy against the Holy Ghost shall not be forgiven unto men. And whosoever speaketh a word against the Son of man, it shall be forgiven him; but whosoever speaketh against the Holy Ghost, it shall not be forgiven him, neither in this world, neither in the world to come." (Matt. xii. 31, 32.) This fearful sin consists in a persevering, wilful, intelligent rejection of salvation, as it has been brought nigh to the soul, by the Spirit enlightening the mind, pricking the heart, alarming the conscience. When a man has thus been impelled to acknowledge the truth and to make a deliberate profession of it, and afterwards turns back, crucifying the Son of God afresh and putting him to an open shame; doing despite to the Spirit of all grace, he turns back unto perdition: he rejects the only possible way of salvation; he tramples under foot the only blood that can take away sin; and he seals his damnation. See Heb. vi. 1–6, and x. 26–29: 1 John v. 16. Stephen charges the mob, "Ye stiff-necked, and uncircumcised in heart and ears—*i. e.* rejecters and haters of the truth—ye do always resist the Holy Ghost." (Acts vii. 51.) The doleful consequences of this sin evince the transcendant dignity of the person and the indispensable necessity of his work. Could it have been said of these persons, "but ye are *washed*, but ye are justified, but ye are *sanctified* in the name of the Lord and by the *Spirit* of our God," this fearful sin could not have been sealed upon their souls. But having persevered in resisting light and knowledge, the plainest proofs of the Messiahship of Christ and the convictions of their own consciences, as stirred up and moved by the Holy Ghost, nothing remained to them, but a certain fearful looking-for of judgment and fiery indignation, which must devour them in Tophet, as adversaries of the Holy Spirit.

Having used this as argument, it may be proper, before leaving it, to throw out a caveat against an unjust and injurious use of this unpardonable sin. People have often taken up the idea that they themselves have committed it, and so write bitter things and make themselves miserable on that supposition. Nothing is more unreasonable and unscriptural. For the sin consists essentially in a hardening process—a callous, dead insensibility and disregard of spiritual things. "Now the Spirit speaketh expressly, that in the latter times some shall depart from the faith, giving heed to seducing spirits, and doctrines of devils; speaking lies in hypocrisy, having their conscience seared with a hot iron." (1 Tim. iv. 1, 2.) If, therefore, a person is perplexed and in distress on account of this fear, he gives, in the very fact, evidence that he has not sinned this sin which hath never forgiveness. For he shows tenderness of conscience and anxiety about his soul's salvation: he displays reverential regard toward the Spirit and his work.

The interview between Christ and Nicodemus, John iii., sets beyond all doubt the question of efficient agency, in reference to the first part of sanctification. The new birth, there ascribed to the Spirit, is in chap. i. 13 ascribed to God. "Which were born, not of blood, nor of the will of the flesh, nor of the will of man, but of God." "The love of God is shed abroad in our hearts by the Holy Ghost, which is given unto us." (Rom. v. 5.)— "That the offering up of the Gentiles might be acceptable, being *sanctified* by the Holy Ghost." (Rom. xv. 16.) But now the shedding of love abroad in the heart, as we shall see, is of the very essence of sanctification, and we are made acceptable unto God by the Spirit's influence and power: "Not by might, nor by power, but by my Spirit, saith the Lord." In 2 Cor. iii. 18, we read, "But we all, with open face beholding as in a glass the glory of the Lord, are changed into the same image from glory to glory, even as by the Spirit of the Lord." Here is progressive sanctification. Farther evidence of the Spirit's work must come up in the next chapter.

CHAPTER VIII.

ON REGENERATION—SANCTIFICATION BEGUN.

"There being in man's spirit by nature no holy thing, it is necessary that the very germ of spiritual life be implanted: the dead soul must be made alive. This is a change from death unto life: not indeed in a natural sense; not in reference to the body; but to the spirit. 'That which is born of the flesh is flesh; and that which is born of the Spirit is spirit.' This doctrine, new and strange to the carnally-minded, was taught from the beginning; and is found in the Old Testament. 'I will take away the hard and stony heart out of your flesh, and will give you a heart of flesh. A new heart will I give unto you, and a right spirit will I put within you.' And many of the typical washings symbolized the same thing." *Junkin on Justification*, p. 334.

"This holy change is wrought by divine power. Our Saviour tells Nicodemus, 'Except a man be born of water and the Spirit he cannot enter into the kingdom of God.' The analogy of a new birth signifies, that it is entirely the work of the sancti-
5

fying Spirit, that conveys a principle of life in order to the functions of life. It is the living impression of God, the sole efficient and exemplar of it, the fruit and image of the divine virtues. It is expressed by the new creature. The production of it is attributed to God's power, displaying itself in a peculiar, excellent way, even in that precise manner, as in making the world. For, as in the first creation, all things were originally of nothing; so in the second, the habit of grace is infused into the soul that was utterly void of it, and in which there was as little preparation for true holiness, as of nothing to produce this great and regular world. And although there is not only an absolute privation of grace, but a fierce resistance against it, yet creating, invincible power does as infallibly produce its effect in forming the new creature, as in making the world. Hence it appears, that renewing grace is entirely the work of God, as his forming the human body from the dust of earth at first; but with this difference, the first creation was without any sense in the subject, of the efficiency of the Divine power in producing it; but in the new creation, man feels the vital influence of the Spirit, applying itself to all his faculties, reforming and enabling them to act according to the quality of their nature." (*Bates's Works*, iii. 417.) Such is the language of the Westminster age, showing that there is no new theory in the theology of our day among evangelical divines.

The nature of this change may be learned from the phraseology by which it is expressed in Scripture.

(a) It is called a new creation. (2 Cor. v. 17.) "Therefore, if any man be in Christ, he is a new creature." (Gal. vi. 15.) "For in Christ Jesus neither circumcision availeth anything, nor uncircumcision, but a new creature." In producing this change, the Holy Ghost puts forth an energy of creating power; just as he did when he breathed into man's nostrils at first the breath of lives. Consequently

(b) It is a passing from death unto life. (1 John iii. 14.) "We know that we have passed from death unto life, because we love the brethren. He that loveth not his brother abideth in death." Observe, *abideth in death;* implying the moral death of the soul; and that in this state it would remain, but for the creating energy of the Spirit. So Col. iii. 3: " For ye are dead, and your life is hid with Christ in God." And Eph. ii. 5: " Even when we were dead in sins, hath he quickened— (made alive) us together with Christ."

(c) Born again—born from above—(John iii. 1–12.) I need not write off this passage. All Bible readers are familiar with it, and i. 13 has been quoted above. (1 John iii. 9:) " Whosoever is born of God doth not commit sin"—and before, (ii. 29.) " Every one that doeth righteousness is born of him." And iv. 7—"Every one that loveth is born of God."

—And v. 1, iv. 18. So 1 Pet. i. 23: "Being born again, not of corruptible seed, but of incorruptible, by the word of God, which liveth and abideth for ever." This oft repeated term is surely intended to describe a very great change in our spiritual man.

(*d*) It is a passing from darkness to light. Col. i. 13: "Who hath delivered us from the power of darkness, and hath translated us into the kingdom of his dear Son." 1 Thes. v. 4, 5: "But ye, brethren, are not in darkness, that that day should overtake you as a thief. Ye are all the children of light, and the children of the day: we are not of the night, nor of darkness." 1 Pet. ii. 9: "That ye should show forth the praises of him who hath called you out of darkness into his marvellous light." Paul (Acts xxvi. 18) describes his mission as appointed "to open their eyes, and to turn them from darkness to light:" and 1 John ii. 9, teaches that " he who hateth his brother is in darkness—and walketh in darkness"—he is in an unregenerate state, and his conduct accords thereto. Paul (Eph. v. 8, 9) thus describes the change: "For ye were sometime darkness, but now are ye light in the Lord. For the fruit of the Spirit is in all goodness, and righteousness, and truth." And all these and other similar passages are given, because "God is light, and in him is no darkness at all."

(*e*) Removing the heart of stone and substituting a heart of flesh. Ezek. xi. 19, and xxxvi. 25,

26, 27: "Then will I sprinkle clean water upon you, and ye shall be clean : from all your filthiness, and from all your idols, will I cleanse you. A new heart also will I give you, and a new spirit will I put within you: and I will take away the stony heart out of your flesh, and I will give you an heart of flesh. And I will put my Spirit within you, and cause you to walk in my statutes, and ye shall keep my judgments, and do them." Here we have first, the promise of the Holy Spirit, under the sign of sprinkling clean water upon you : parallel with Isa. xliv. 3, "For I will pour water upon him that is thirsty, and floods upon the dry ground ; I will pour my Spirit upon thy seed, and my blessings upon thine offspring." Thus the baptism of the Holy Ghost is pointed out, and the manner of it —by sprinkling or pouring upon the subject. Then, in v. 27, this sprinkling is expounded of the Spirit. Then 3dly, we notice the effects of this Spirit poured, a new heart of flesh bestowed and the heart of stone removed—regeneration. Then 4thly, practical holiness—walking in my statutes. The same nearly in Ps. li. 10 : " Create in me a clean heart, O God ; and renew a right spirit within me."

(*f*) A change from enmity to love. Compare Rom. viii. 7—" The carnal mind is enmity against God ; for it is not subject to the law of God, neither indeed can be," with v. 5,—" Because the love of God is shed abroad in our hearts by the Holy Ghost, which is given unto us." Nor is there any power but he, that can destroy the carnal enmity and fill the soul with love to God and to his children: wherever, therefore, this change is effected, there we have a work of the Holy Spirit.

(*g*) Perhaps there is a little inaccuracy in so doing, yet will we place the change of the will in this class. Opposition of will in man toward God is obviously characteristic of his natural state. Ye will not come to me that ye might have life. Turn ye, turn ye, why *will* ye die? God reveals his will as the rule of man's action, and man wilfully moves in the opposite direction. Now the Scriptures speak of a people being subdued. Addressing the Messiah, the Psalmist (cx. 2) says, "The Lord shall send the rod of thy strength out of Zion; rule thou in the midst of thine enemies." The governing authority of Messiah shall be exercised even among his enemies; and the consequence is described in the next verse—"Thy people shall be willing in the day of thy power, in the beauties of holiness from the womb of the morning; thou hast the dew of thy youth." The people voluntarily offer themselves as free-will offerings unto Zion's Priest-king. More distinctly is the idea expressed in Phil. ii. 13: "For it is God which worketh in you both to will and to do of his good pleasure." A divine energy is put forth for the renewing of our wills. And Heb. xiii. 21 contains the same: "Now the God of peace make you perfect in every good work, working in you that which is well-pleasing in his sight, through Jesus Christ." The disposition—the inclination of will, is the result of his working in you. Let these suffice to give us an idea of the general nature of regeneration from the *phraseology of Scripture*.

2. The nature of this change may be further ascertained from its sequences. Effects indicate the nature of their producing cause; and we may reason both ways, either from causes forward to their effects, or from effects backward to their causes. But as we will have occasion for this, when we come to inquire for the evidences of regeneration, it will be profitable to postpone this evidence of change until that subject comes up in course.

3. Regeneration is an instantaneous change. It is not like Sanctification, (of which it is a part,) complex, and successive; but the immediate effect of a single act. One moment the soul is dead; and the next it is alive: "It is entirely," says Dr. Bates, "the work of the sanctifying Spirit, that conveys a principle of life in order to the functions of it." Where there is no natural life, there is no natural action; so, where there is no spiritual life, there is no spiritual action. Give the principle, and you shall have the practice: supply the faculty, and you shall have the function. When the command issued, "Lazarus, come forth," the creating energy of the Spirit re-produced the life; the vital functions were instantly exerted. This brings us

into close proximity with another position, whose discussion can scarcely be held separate from this, and we will save time and not create confusion, by starting another point, viz.

4. That the soul is passive in regeneration. Our spirit is the subject of the change; and not, in any correct sense, the agent in its production. By this we do not mean, that man's spirit is like a marble block under the hand and chisel of the sculptor, which has no motion whatever, or capacity to move and act. On the contrary, we know the soul to be active in many respects. The intellect, the understanding, the reason, the emotions and passions, are all in operation before and up to the moment when the new life is generated, and they continue so afterwards. But then, it is not any of these activities; nor all of them combined, that generate this new life—this new creation. The power that causes it, is not in them, but in God the Holy Ghost. All that goes to prove the Spirit's exclusive activity, also demonstrates the soul's *passivity* —to use a term invented by the opposers of our doctrine. The apostle, Eph. ii. 1, says, "You were dead in trespasses and sins." But proceeds instantly to speak of their activity in that dead condition. "Wherein in time past ye walked according to the course of this world, according to the prince of the power of the air, the spirit that now worketh in the children of disobedience: among whom also we all had our conversation in times past

in the lusts of our flesh, fulfilling the desires of the flesh and of the mind: and were by nature the children of wrath, even as others." Notwithstanding this strenuous and energetic activity in the service of Satan, "we were dead in sins," and so the proper subjects of regenerating power, v. 5. "Even when we were dead in sins, God hath *quickened* us together with Christ,"—*brought us to life*. Now this quickening by the Spirit—this making the soul alive, is inconceivable, is impossible, if the death in sin did not before exist. The instantaneousness of the change may easily be conceived and believed, from its nature, and also from the apostle's assertion, as to the resurrection of the body, and the change of those who shall be found on the earth—"In a moment, in the twinkling of an eye, at the last trump." (1 Cor. xv. 52.) If the dead matter in the graves, and the living men above ground can be so suddenly changed, how much more the dead souls.

Moreover, let the objector make the effort, to conceive the spiritual life of the soul to be gradually produced; and that partly by its own activity; and let him raise the question,—but what if the process were suspended exactly in the middle? Can he conceive of a soul half-regenerated? A spirit half-born! A man possessed of half a spiritual life!! The absurdity of these half-born, half-life twin conceptions, may convince him, that in reality he denies regeneration altogether, and occupies the ground of Dr. Paley, who says—"There may be Christians, who are, and have been, in such a religious state, that no such thorough and radical change, as is usually meant by conversion, is or was necessary for them ; and that they need not be made miserable by the want of consciousness of such a change." (*Paley's Works*, iv. 167.) This is daubing with untempered mortar. See Ezek. xiii. 10 and xxii. 28.

It is therefore untrue, as some affirm, that a man has as much ability to change his own heart as to split a log of wood, is as active in the one case as in the other: or. that sanctification is a series of holy acts, and regeneration is the first act of the series. These are soul-destroying errors; and amount to a rejection of the entire scheme of salvation by free grace.

CHAPTER IX.

THE NECESSITY OF REGENERATION.

A THING may be absolutely or conditionally necessary. An absolute necessity is, when it could not and cannot be otherwise. Under no possible or supposable state of things could it be different from what it is. Perhaps in this high and bold sense, God's being and incommunicable attributes may be said to be the only absolute necessities. No human mind can conceive the non-existence of God; or of any of his essential attributes. The fool indeed hath said, there is no God; but he said it "in his heart;" it was his corrupt lusts that dictated the expression. His intellect never conceived its truth; his understanding never believed it.

A conditional necessity is, when a thing must be in order to the existence of something else. We express it commonly by the word *must*. On the condition or hypothesis that I am to live in the enjoyment of health and comfort, I *must*—*i. e.* it is *necessary* for me to eat wholesome food. We express the condition very commonly by the word *if*. If the ship's passengers are to be saved, these sailors *must*—it is *necessary* for them to abide in the ship. If thou wilt have life, keep the commandments. Life is the reward of obedience, this, therefore, is the condition of life. This is what Edwards calls a necessity of consequence. The relation between the two things is such, that the one must and will follow the other. There is between them an unknown and mysterious connection, which we designate by the words *cause* and *effect*—or *causality*. But we are totally ignorant what it is. The most we can make of it, is the mere verbal expression or definition—*cause is uniform and necessary antecedent; effect is uniform and necessary consequent*. But let the simple-hearted reader know, that this definition is a mere subterfuge, under which the metaphysician conceals his ignorance. We do not understand what this principle of causality is. Facing the question of conditional necessity, with this bit of metaphysics in his hand, he will soon find that to be necessary, which sustains the relation of antecedent or cause, to some certain other thing.

Now the Saviour assures Nicodemus, that *to be born again*, is a necessary condition to entering into the kingdom of God. The new birth is not an absolute necessity: for the sinner may go down to hell. But on the hypothesis that he is to enter the gates of glory, his regeneration is indispensable—" Ye must be born again ;" this is the indispensable antecedent. Such is the relation or connection between these two things, as established of God, that if a person is born again, he will certainly enter the kingdom of heaven. Let the antecedent be and the consequent must be.

Now although we know so little about the principles of causality, as to be obliged to resolve it ultimately into the will of God; yet can we go a step behind this, in the present case, and show, in the deep depravity and consequent incompetency of man to enjoy spiritual things, why this conditional necessity exists. In reference to the Holy One of Israel, we can perceive why, both as to his holiness and his justice, this change must be. On the score of holiness, obviously it would be inconsistent to receive a polluted creature into the society of the holy. On that of justice, for God to treat the sinful rebel, with all his rebellious spirit still in him, as though he were an obedient child, would be to abandon righteousness and relinquish the moral government of the universe. "Shall not the Judge of all the earth do right?" To abhor sin and its pollution is a necessity absolute, existing in the nature of God: and this constitutes the basis of the conditioned necessity expressed by the term "must be born again." To enter the kingdom with this guilt and pollution upon him, is an absolute impossibility. The nature of the holy God and the nature of the unholy man are contradictory, and can never agree. "What concord hath Christ with Belial?" One or the other must be changed, and, God being immutable, the change must be made in man.

Moreover, as it regards man himself; supposing all objections waived on the part of God; and the door of heaven thrown open to sinners, with all their corruptions still on them, welcome to enter; still the change must take place. For manifestly, in the society of the pure and the holy and just; the impure and the unholy and unjust could not dwell. Even here, where sanctification, in the best estate, is very imperfect, unregenerate men do not find themselves happy in the society of godly persons. The elements of their life do not, and cannot flow in symphony and tune with the sons and the songs of Zion. How very difficult it is, to bring them into the very imperfectly purified atmosphere of the church militant, our half-filled though beautiful houses of worship, our prayer-meetings and religious conferences, abundantly testify; and how then could they breathe the pure air of heaven, where holiness dwells; and the spirits of the just made perfect tune their harps to praise redeeming love? Thus we and they are thrown back upon the awful, yet blessed truth,

"The sinner must be born again,
Or drink the wrath of God."

CHAPTER X.

REGENERATION MYSTERIOUS—OBJECTIONS.

If this change is a creation, it must be mysterious. A creature cannot comprehend the exercise of creating power. The production of something out of nothing is perhaps understood by the producer himself alone. Hence the adage, *Ex nihilo, nihil fit*—out of nothing, nothing is made. And to the ancients, ignorant of the true God, it is not at all strange that this should appear a proverbial truth. Accustomed to reason from effects back to their causes; and familiarized with the process of inferring the nature of antecedents in the physical or material world, from their consequents, they could not avoid establishing the rule of proportion, and maintaining that like causes produce like effects; or reversely, like effects proceed from like causes. This was obvious enough, and very beneficial within the sphere of mere material phenomena. But when they were forced to rove beyond the world of matter; when its very existence became an inquiry; ignorant of any adequate cause of its production many assumed its eternity, and from the maxim,

Ex nihilo, nihil fit, some denied that it had any cause: others, unwilling to acknowledge the inadequacy of their philosophy, ran into wild speculations about the origin of the world; which are of some use to us, inasmuch as they show the earnest yearnings of the soul after a knowledge too mysterious for its unaided comprehension. Now, this plodding and floundering of the human intellect, in vain search of an adequate first cause; or, in other words, of a creating power, proves the operations of such power to be among the deep things of God. If he did nothing, but what man's feeble intellect could perfectly comprehend and fully explain, he could not command the respect and adoration of his creatures. But he is wonderful in counsel and mighty in working. "I will praise thee; for I am fearfully and wonderfully made; marvellous are thy works; and that my soul knoweth right well." (Ps. cxxxix. 14.) "He holdeth back the face of his throne, and spreadeth his cloud upon it. He hath compassed the waters with bounds, until the day and night come to an end. The pillars of heaven tremble, and are astonished at his reproof. He divideth the sea with his power, and by his understanding he smiteth through the proud. By his Spirit he hath garnished the heavens; his hand hath formed the crooked serpent. Lo, these are parts of his ways; but how little a portion is heard of him? but the thunder of his power who can understand?" (Job xxvi. 9–14.) "As thou knowest not what is the way of the Spirit, nor how the bones do grow in the womb of her that is with child: even so thou knowest not the works of God who maketh all things." (Eccl. xi. 5.) Incomprehensibility as to the mode, is an obvious characteristic of creating power. And therefore our ignorance of the mode, is no better argument against the fact of regeneration, than it is against the fact of generation.

And yet this is the first and most obvious objection. "*How* can a man be born when he is old?" Even so earnest and sincere a seeker as Nicodemus felt the difficulty. "*How* can these things be?" Manifestly the mode in which the change is effected is the very point of his difficulty. And it is equally manifest that the "Teacher come from God" does not meet this precise point. He does not attempt to explain the method and manner of the Spirit's operation. All he insists on is the *fact—ye must be born again;* and then exposes the unphilosophicalness of the objection.

Did our Saviour blench before an objector and evade a direct answer to the precise point of the difficulty? Did he shrink from an objection by an anxious inquirer, and refuse to give the information best calculated to relieve him? Nay: but he held him up to the exact relief needed. A new life in his soul was the pressing, felt necessity, of this master of Israel, and he is instantly and perseveringly referred to the only source whence it could be obtained. The *how*—the *quomodo* is not attempted, for the simple reason, that even the cultivated mind of this educated man, could not be made to understand the mode of a Divine creative influence: and farther, because the knowledge, if possible, would be unavailing. A new heart was the crying necessity, and not any abstruse theory of life-generation.

The unreasonableness of objecting on the ground of ignorance as to the mode of the Spirit's influence, he then exposes. "The wind bloweth where it listeth, and thou hearest the sound thereof, but canst not tell whence it cometh, and whither it goeth; so is every one that is born of the Spirit." Here is a natural phenomenon, perfectly familiar, and yet the mode of this familiar fact lies hidden from you. The winds and the sea are all regulated and controlled by Divine power, but do you know how? If then, the fact of the wind's motions, as it is exhibited in providence, is obvious, and yet you know not the modes of its movements, why should it not be so also with the fact of the Spirit's power in new-creating the soul? You avail yourself of the wind—you breathe it and receive its beneficial effects in purifying the element in which you live, but understand not whence it cometh and whither it goeth, why should it be otherwise with the Spirit, when he breathes into the soul the breath of a new life? "So is every one that is born of the Spirit."

The modes of Divine influence and power are

equally inscrutable, all over the material world, the spiritual world, and the commixture of the two in man's nature. In the conflicts between the infidel geologists and other votaries of natural science and Christianity, the latter has yielded too much to the assumption, that the modes of influence in physical laws are understood. This is not true. The natural philosopher is as entirely ignorant of the mode of antecedence and consequence, called the law of gravitation, as is the Christian philosopher in regard to the mode of the Divine influence in regeneration. And thus is it with all that are called laws of nature. The forms of their expression merely intimate an order of actual sequence; they make no pretension, unless in the hands of mere sciolists, to explain what causality is, or how cause and effect are linked together. When, therefore, the apostle (1 Cor. xv. 51) says, "Behold, I show you a mystery. We shall not all sleep, but we shall all be changed," he announces nothing peculiar to spiritual science. Similar mysteries abound in the physical world; and in the metaphysical. Who professes to tell us how the soul and body of man influence one another? how the image of the object presented to the eye reaches the mind? What engineer has undertaken to build a bridge across the chasm between ontology and pneumatology—the world of matter and the world of mind? Let naturalists then acknowledge that their field of philosophizing is full of unexplained mysteries; and let all men cease their objection to the doctrine of regeneration, because its mode is a mystery.

What does the Spirit do in this change?—we are sometimes asked, what addition does he make to the soul; what faculty has the regenerated which does not exist in the unregenerate? Is there any new faculty added?

The answer to this objection will depend very much on the meaning attached to the word faculty. If it mean an organic power, such as the faculty of sight, hearing, smelling, tasting, feeling; then we deny that such organic power or faculty is given in regeneration. Even a blind man is not restored to sight, when he is born again. The deaf ears are not physically unstopped. But if by faculty be meant an ability, capacity, or power to do acts for which there was no power before; then we affirm such faculty is given in the new creation. Old things are passed away, all things are become new. There is superadded in the regenerate, a faculty of spiritual discernment. 1 Cor. ii. 14: "But the natural man—the unregenerate—receiveth not the things of the Spirit of God, for they are foolishness unto him: neither can he know them, because they are spiritually discerned. But he that is spiritual judgeth all things." Here is a new power added, a faculty given which he had not before. The change in the man born blind and restored to sight by our Lord is not set forth in more decided and distinct terms. Beyond doubt, the case of the blind man is intended to illustrate the subject of regeneration; and it forms a beautiful illustration of our answer to the objection against mystery in the mode. The Pharisees harassed, and tried to distract the poor man, by raising this difficulty. What did he do unto thee? How did he open thine eyes? The simple response constantly was, "He put clay upon mine eyes and I washed, and do see." Their pertinacious pressing upon him of the question of mode, shows how they were galled by the simplicity of the truth. And the indifference of the happy man as to the mode, while he held on to the fact, is instructive. "Whether he be a sinner I know not; but one thing I know, that whereas I was blind, now I see." Little care I as to the manner of my power of vision; I see, that satisfies me.

CHAPTER XI.

EVIDENCES OF REGENERATION.

THAT a change so great should take place, in a mind conscious to itself of living powers, and yet make no revelation of itself in the consciousness of that mind, it were difficult to believe. Especially, when the change is the creation of a new life-principle of incessant activity, it is hardly conceivable that it should lie hidden and unknown in the bosom. On the contrary, it is most reasonable to expect this new and active principle and power, to work itself into notice; and, by the display of its activities to evince the reality of its being. What then are the evidences of regeneration? Without professing to furnish a full and perfect response, let us note the following.

1. A general modification of views in the mind—old things pass away and all things become new. And here we must have some minor detail.

(*a*) The intellectual perceptions of the law of God and of the gospel of his grace are remodelled. The law formerly appeared a severe rule indeed, but addressed to external things and requiring outward compliance; and so not extremely difficult of fulfilment. "All these have I kept from my youth up." "I was alive without the law once"— alive,—confident and bold in the belief that I had lived up to its requirements. Now, "I have seen an end of all perfection, but thy commandment is exceeding broad"—when it came in its breadth and spirituality, "sin revived and I died." I saw it legislated to the heart and required the subjection of all the inner man. The gospel too appears a different thing. Formerly it was a mere temporary aid to my supposed and almost complete good works; a new rule, slightly modified, in kind condescension to my slight imperfection—a new law of grace, requiring sincere, although not absolutely perfect obedience: now, it is no relaxation of law, but comes with a full and perfect satisfaction to all its claims, and points out clearly how this fulness becomes available. Not one jot or tittle does it abate, of the most complete fulfilment of law. But all this not by my doings, but the Saviour's works.

(*b*) The world's pleasures—the earth's wealth and grandeur have undergone a great change. I see through a new medium that alters the aspect of the whole. Its distinctions, its honours, its gilded glories, its civic ambitions, its military glare and blood-stained triumphs—all these how changed! My understanding weighs their worth in the balances of the sanctuary, and the judgments of the mind make them but very little things. "What is a man profited if he shall gain the whole world and yet lose his own soul?"

(c) Views of the Redeemer are different. Before he was as a root out of a dry ground, having no form, nor comeliness; and when I beheld him, there was no beauty in him, that I should desire him. After this change, he rises before my eyes all glorious, having no spot or wrinkle—the rose of Sharon, the lily of the valley—yea, he is altogether lovely.

(d) The material world all around appears different. Formerly indeed, the beauties of nature were a source of enjoyment. I could feast my eyes for long hours, strolling over the flower garden, the green meadow, the bending harvest field, the distant woods, the towering mountains—the grand and glorious starry firmament. But alas! how little did I see of God in the flower, the field, the woodlands, the towering mountains, or even the starry expanse! How little did I see of him in the clouds or hear in the wind! How little headway did I make, in reasoning up through nature unto nature's God! But now, lo, how changed! All nature is full of God—the God of justice and the God of grace. I see him in the snow white lily; in the crimson streaks of the tulip, painted by his own hand; in the modest rose, that blushes to behold its Maker: I see him opening his bountiful hand in the golden waves of the wheat lands; in the rich rustling green of the corn fields; in the exuberance of the garden; in the bloom and the pendent burdens of the orchard; his voice I hear in the moaning waves of the majestic forest; in the cloud and thunder of the distant mountain; I see him in the mystic dance of the planetary world and the music of the spheres; I trace his footsteps above the stars of God, and behold him as the Sun of righteousness upon the throne of his glory. Oh, yes: *now*, that his own bright light shines upon my soul, I can reason up through nature unto nature's God.

2. The emotional states are different from their former selves—the feelings are changed. Emotions are dependent upon the intellectual states, and, consequently, when these change so must those. That the heart be changed, and yet its feelings remain the same, is an impossibility, very nearly related to an absurdity. If the enmity is slain—the carnal mind crucified, the general current of feeling must change. There may remain some evil affections; but there must be those that are good. If the tree is made good, the fruit will be so too. If the fountain is purified, pure waters will flow from it. Two classes of feelings cover the whole ground —those of attachment and love; and those of aversion and hate. The renewed mind turns away from the very objects of its former regard; and turns toward those it formerly despised. And here we must arrest this discussion, for it runs us into the general subject of repentance, which merits a chapter for itself.

3. Habitual inclination of thoughts and feelings

in the right direction proves the mind and heart to have been renewed. Where our heart is, it is exceedingly probable our "treasure will be also." "For our conversation—our habitual course of action—is in heaven; whence also we look for the Saviour, the Lord Jesus Christ:" Phil. iii. 20. "If ye then be risen with Christ, seek those things which are above, where Christ sitteth on the right hand of God:" Col. iii. 1. If our thoughts carry us, as it were by stealth, away after heavenly things, it is certainly a favourable sign. "Or ever I was aware, my soul made me as the chariots of Amminadib:" Can. vi. 12. To the renewed mind heavenly things are the main objects of desire—the treasure; they are the point of attraction, and whenever released from earthly influences, which draw it aside from heavenly contemplation, the mind returns to this point—

—"In every clime, the magnet of his soul,
Touched by remembrance, trembles to that pole."

This too occurs in our slumbering moments. When half awake and half asleep—which is the region of dream-land—we find thoughts of God and heaven intruding themselves into the chambers of the half-open consciousness, it indicates the habitual bent of the soul. "For a dream cometh through the multitude of business," and this class of dreams so coming, are influenced by the trains of waking thoughts, and manifest their direction.

"They that are after the flesh do mind the things of the flesh, and they that are after the Spirit the things of the Spirit."

4. Nearly allied to the foregoing, is the saying of John, before quoted: "We know that we have passed from death unto life, because we love the brethren:" 1 John iii. 14. This is exceedingly simple, and of easy application. Am I a child of God? If so, his other children must be objects of my affectionate regard. Whenever and wherever I see the lineaments of the family countenance, I must find an object for filial affection. He that loveth him that begat, loveth him also that is begotten of him. If we wish to see the reason of this evidence, we have only to inquire, what is the state of feeling, in the unrenewed mind, toward the holy ones of God. "If the world hate you, ye know that it hated me before it hated you. If ye were of the world, the world would love his own; but because ye are not of the world, but I have chosen you out of the world, therefore the world hateth you:" John xv. 18, 19. But we all were of the world once; and were by nature the children of wrath even as others. "For we ourselves were sometimes foolish, disobedient, deceived, serving diverse lusts and pleasures, living in malice and envy, hateful and hating one another:" Tit. iii. 3. Consequently, if now we love the brethren, a change must have been wrought in us; and we know that the love of God is shed abroad in our hearts, by the

Holy Ghost, which is given to us. Thus the evidence is conclusive.

But some may inquire, how can I know that I love the brethren? How do you know that you love your husband, your wife, the child of your bosom, your father, your mother, your sister, your brother? How? Why, by the inner conscious activities of your heart, striving ever to do good to the object of your love: and by this outward embodiment of it in deeds of kindness. All, therefore, dear reader, that is wanting to the fulness of this proof, is to look within and discover there true love to the children of God. You will, of course, surely not mistake sectarian zeal for Christian charity. You will not substitute hatred for other sects, in place of love for Christians. You will not inquire, does he belong to us? Is he a Presbyterian? a Methodist? a Baptist, an Episcopalian? But simply is he a Christian? Is he a child of God, a brother of Jesus? Then, with an affirmative answer, you throw the arms of your love around him, and feel that you yourself too are a child of God and an heir of glory: that as you love him that is begotten of him, you are of the same blessed household of faith and love.

5. Love to God dwells in the hearts of all that are begotten of him. Regeneration is described in Col. iii. 9, 10, as a putting off of the old man, with his deeds, and a putting on of the new man, which is renewed in knowledge after the image of

him that created him." Now God is love, and he that dwelleth in love dwelleth in God and God in him: nor is there a more prominent characteristic of the Divine image than this, "for love is of God; and every one that loveth is born of God, and knoweth God." The same course of remark, as under the last evidence, is applicable here, and we need not repeat it. Only one turn to the thought may be added: viz. that on the secondary question, Do I love the Lord? we have this simple test; Do I keep his commandments? "If ye love me, keep my commandments." The existence of love to God, where formerly there was only the enmity and hate of the carnal mind, is proof indubitable of a total change: and the Spirit of obedience, leading to constant efforts to fulfil the law, proves the existence and genuineness of this love. But, as this last point will come before us in another relation, we waive it for the present.

6. The witness of the Holy Spirit establishes the fact of regeneration. "For ye have not received the spirit of bondage again to fear; but ye have received the Spirit of adoption, whereby we cry Abba, Father. The Spirit itself beareth witness with our spirit, that we are the children of God." Rom. viii. 15, 16. It is by his witness-bearing, that he becomes the Spirit of adoption, in which he gives in the soul practical and satisfactory evidence of our change of heart. In reference to this conjunct testimony of the Spirit of God and of our own

souls, there is room for some variety of opinion, but chiefly there are two explanations. One is, that the Holy Ghost operates directly and immediately with and upon our souls, not using any instrumentalities in this work, other than those preparatory to the regenerating act. Thus, our spirit has an immediate knowledge—a knowledge of its change, not through any medium whatever. This, if I understand the idea, is not distinguishable from regeneration itself: but is involved in it: the evidence and the thing of which it is the evidence seem to run together and become identical. The witness-bearing is as mysterious and as inexplicable as the life-giving act itself. The safety of this view I doubt. It is in great danger of running into wild superstition—hallucination, ecstasies and raptures. Very probably it lies at the foundation of an error in regard to the time of regeneration. If the change—and his knowledge of it, are cotemporaneous, as seems to be the conception, then, it must follow, that every person could tell the very day and hour of his new birth: a superstition that has often disturbed the church and distracted and distressed many minds. As well might you deny a man's natural birth, unless he could remember the hour of its occurrence.

The other view makes the conjunct witnessing, subsequent to and distinct in time and manner, from the change itself. It presupposes the permanent inhabitation of the Spirit in the believer. It assumes, as the text teaches, two distinct witnesses conjointly testifying to the truth of the same fact. To this the phraseology leads us. It must mean our Spirit as renewed; and its witness must be after regeneration and not cotemporaneous with it. This view avoids the danger above alluded to. It makes this conjoint witnessing a work, and not simply an act. It therefore requires time and the inhabitation of the Spirit, and so belongs not to regeneration properly, but, being subsequent to it, must be referred to its proper place, in the progressive work of sanctification.

CHAPTER XII.

THE INHABITATION OF THE SPIRIT.

THE Holy Ghost, as God, is omnipresent. There is no point in space from which he is absent. "Whither shall I go from thy Spirit, or whither shall I flee from thy presence? If I ascend up into heaven, thou art there: if I make my bed in hell, (the grave or the invisible world,) behold, thou art there. If I take the wings of the morning, and dwell in the uttermost parts of the sea; even there shall thy hand lead me, and thy right hand shall hold me:" Psalm cxxxix. 7-17. But this omnipresence of the Spirit is not what the Scriptures mean by the *indwelling* or *inhabitation*. True it is, he is thus present in our inmost being, and therefore he is privy to our most secret thoughts. But thus he is present to all beings, good and bad. The inhabitation, however, of which we speak, is a different matter in some respects: it indeed includes this omnipresence; but it goes much farther. He is, in a very peculiar manner, the inhabitant of the body and the spirit of the regenerated. "What! know ye not that your body is the temple of the Holy

Ghost, which is in you, which ye have of God, and ye are not your own? For ye are bought with a price: therefore glorify God in your body, and in your spirit, which are God's:" 1 Cor. vi. 19, 20. The allusion seems to be to an item of common traffic. A man purchases a house, moves his family and goods into it, and there takes up his permanent abode. The dwelling and all its appurtenances are his own, and he has the right of undisturbed occupancy and use. This is a very different matter from a man's sojourning in the house of another; or of "the way-faring man, who turneth in to tarry for the night," and is gone by the morning light. Thus also the Saviour discourses in his long address at the first sacramental supper, "And I will pray the Father, and he shall give you another Comforter, that he may abide with you for ever; even the Spirit of truth; whom the world cannot receive, because it seeth him not; neither knoweth him; but ye know him; for he dwelleth with you, and shall be in you:" John xiv. 16, 17. So in 1 John ii. 27: "But the anointing which ye have received of him abideth in you, and ye need not that any man teach you; but as the same anointing teacheth you of all things,"&c. So in Rom. viii. 9–11: "But ye are not in the flesh, (in a state of unregeneracy,) but in the Spirit, if so be that the Spirit of God dwell in you. Now, if any man have not the Spirit of Christ, he is none of his. And if Christ be in you, the body is dead because of sin; but the spirit is life because of righteousness. But if the Spirit of him that raised up Jesus from the dead dwell in you, he that raised up Christ from the dead shall also quicken your mortal bodies by his Spirit that dwelleth in you." This personal in-being is begun, when the Spirit, being sent from the Father, at the supplication of the Son, commences a work of conviction to terminate in conversion and sanctification: and must be distinguished from occasional influences exerted by him in the conscience, whereby the soul is partially aroused and alarmed; but which prove evanescent and temporary. Such are deplored by the prophet. "Oh, the Hope of Israel, the Saviour thereof in time of trouble, why shouldest thou be as a stranger in the land, and as a way-faring man that turneth aside to tarry for a night?" Jer. xiv. 8.

These occasional visits, it is greatly feared, are often mistaken for gracious operations; and are thereby improved, by the grand adversary, as a means of lulling the soul to the entertainment of false hopes and fatal security. Not so, when a work of grace is to be begun and carried on: then this indwelling—this personal, operating presence, of the Holy Ghost, is fixed and unchangeable: the person of the subject becomes a temple of the Lord, and in it he abideth for ever. "I will never leave thee, nor forsake thee:" Heb. xiii. 5: "Know ye not that ye are the temple of God, and that the

Spirit of God, dwelleth in you. If any man defile the temple of God, him shall God destroy : for the temple of God is holy, which temple ye are:" 1 Cor. iii. 16, 17. Now, that he has taken up his permanent abode in this temple, and begun the work of its purification in creating it anew, the Holy Ghost proceeds toward its perfection.

CHAPTER XIII.

ON SAVING FAITH.

This caption suggests at sight the idea, that there is a faith which does not save the soul. And this, alas! is true to an alarming extent. James speaks of a dead faith, that is common to deceived and deceitful men, and to fallen angels. "Even so faith, if it hath not works, is dead, being alone. Thou believest that there is one God; thou doest well: the devils also believe, and tremble:" Jas. ii. 17-19.

For the right understanding of this whole matter, let us advert to the general principle. Faith is reliance on testimony. It is a natural principle of the mind, an element innate, or con-created with us; an essential attribute of our being, without which we would not be men and could not be rational and accountable agents. There is no part of our being more extensively useful and more indispensable to be used than the law of belief—the disposition to receive and rest upon the testimony of other intelligent and rational beings. It is not the result of experience, as Hume assumes, but an original law, anterior to all experience. Every human being, we might amplify and say every rational being, is predisposed to receive as true whatever is testified unto by another. And so far from faith or belief being an acquired habit—the result of experience derived from observing that one and another and another has told us the truth; unbelief, distrust, refusal to receive as true, whatever others have testified, is the acquisition of experience. All men naturally believe what is told them, until they learn, by sad experience, that some men will lie: and generally it requires us to be often deceived by falsehoods, before we can school ourselves into a due and necessary degree of caution. Childhood is the period of the simplest belief, and this simplicity of confidence is the leading and prominent characteristic of children. They believe all that is told to them, until, discovering falsehood, they learn to doubt. Now, it is to this characteristic the Saviour refers, when he says, "Except ye be converted and become as little children, ye shall not enter into the kingdom of heaven:" Matthew xviii. 3.

This natural law of belief has for its direct object, veracity in the testifier; it accredits him as a man of truth that will not lie; and refusal to do this is an accusation and charge of falsehood, and exceedingly offensive. Hence the reason of the fact, that few things so fire up a man's indignation as the questioning of his veracity. It is a virtual declaration of his unfitness for human society; for, obviously, without faith in testimony, society could not exist. Such insult was offered, at a very early period in our history, to the Author of our existence, by the creature of his hand. God had testified, "In the day thou eatest thereof, thou shalt surely die." Satan testified, "Ye shall not surely die." Here are two testifiers and two testimonies in direct contradiction to each other; both cannot be true; which will Adam believe?—to which will he append his seal, recognizing his veracity?—and to which will he affix the stigma of falsehood? Manifestly, then, unbelief goes into the very essence of Adam's first sin. He believed that old serpent the devil; he disbelieved the God of truth and righteousness.

Yet this fearful iniquity did not annihilate the natural law of belief; but it brought spiritual death instantly upon the soul of man; blinded his understanding; corrupted his heart; and so disabled him utterly from discerning spiritual things; and thus rendered faith in God, as a spiritual exercise, impossible. Now regeneration restores this faith. It is "through sanctification of the Spirit and belief of the truth," that the grace of faith is reproduced in the soul of man. This reproduction is purely gratuitous and gracious. Never had man returned to confidence in God, but for the creation anew in Christ Jesus. The law of belief is reinstated in his soul, as at the beginning; but with this important appendix, that its continued existence and operation are guarantied by the infallible suretiship of the second Adam. "By grace are ye saved, through faith; and that not of yourselves; it is the gift of God."

In the matter of salvation from death as a punishment for sin; and of justification which secures life eternal by constituting us righteous in Christ, this faith is prominent. In exercising it, the soul sets to its seal that God is true, in his proffer of forgiveness through the efficacy of the atonement or satisfaction made to Divine justice by the sufferings of Christ; and in the proffer of eternal life as the reward of the righteousness of Christ imputed to us; and it is in this peculiar relation it is called *saving* faith. But we are not to suppose, therefore, that faith concerns only our legal relations; in which matter we have no direct concern with it in this treatise. On the contrary, it is in perpetual requisition and constant activity during the whole process of sanctification. Thus Peter, in his address in the synod of Jerusalem, advocates the admission of the Gentiles into the church, on the ground that the Holy Ghost "put no difference between us and them, purifying their hearts by faith:" Acts xv. 9. And Paul speaks of faith, "which worketh by love." And James insists, chap. ii. on faith working, showing that faith is saving, within the sphere of sanctification, as really as in the matter of justification. In truth, faith is indispensable to every Christian duty. He that cometh unto God must believe that he is; and that he is a rewarder of them that diligently seek him; and without faith it is impossible to please God. Even the doctrines of salvation are unprofitable, until they are mixed with faith in them that hear them. And the biography of faith, recorded in the eleventh of Hebrews, is a splendid testimony of its mighty power in all ages of the old dispensation; and it ought to be distinctly noticed, that little attention is given to the first exercises, which secure justification; but the cases relate chiefly to the progress of sanctification.

Again, we remark, the exercise of faith in God is a duty of the law of nature. We cannot even conceive of a moral creature being released from his obligations of trust and confidence in his Maker. No inability, we have seen, cancels moral bonds. Sin is never its own excuse; a man cannot take advantage of and profit by his own wrong-doing. Rebellion against a righteous government can never be right; and it never can cease to be the duty of such a rebel to return to his allegiance. No statute of limitation has ever been passed by the supreme Legislator, fixing a period in duration at and after which the revolted subjects of his empire shall be released from all obligations to return and submit themselves to his righteous government. And so we find the duty of believing pressed upon all men; and the form of the gospel call involves this idea; it is mandatory. Believe in God—believe on the Lord Jesus Christ, and thou shalt be saved. The command to believe is based in the indestructible obligations of law; and is equally binding upon all moral creatures; the promise appended is peculiarly gospel, and emanates from the boundless loving-kindness of the Lord. In the order of nature, it is dependent on the previous command. When the command is obeyed by the individual, which never can be, unless grace in regeneration changes the heart; then the pledged word of the promiser guarantees to the believer the thing promised, and it will be given.

CHAPTER XIV.

ON REPENTANCE UNTO LIFE.

THE soul, which is passive in regeneration, is ever active afterwards. This life principle, like every other, shows itself by its activity. In the fiducial trust in God it is active, and this continues through life. In turning from sin to holiness—from the service of Satan to that of the living God, it is active. Nor can any intelligent creature, that has turned away in rebellion against its Creator, ever annul the obligation to return. Lost men, and fallen angels, are equally under the authority of the God who made them; and are equally bound to return to allegiance. As we stated above—the idea, that their indisposition and inability makes them independent of the Divine government, is not to be tolerated; for it subverts everything like morality, and makes sin its own justification. If, therefore, repentance is a turning from sin to holiness—from rebellion to submission, it is a duty of the moral law, and can never be abrogated. Accordingly we find the Scriptures everywhere enforcing it as a command. Turn you

—let the wicked forsake his ways, and the unrighteous man his thoughts, and let him return unto the Lord—Repent, and believe the gospel—" Repent, and turn yourselves from all your transgressions." It is mandatory.

But, as we have seen, this duty has become, through our own wickedness, impossible: and therefore, if we ever perform it, grace must be given. Thus, " Repentance unto life is a saving grace, wrought in the heart of a sinner by the Spirit and word of God." For this end Peter tells us, " Him hath God exalted with his right hand, to be a Prince and a Saviour, for to *give* repentance to Israel and forgiveness of sins:" Acts v. 31. And xi. 18: " Then hath God also to the Gentiles *granted* repentance unto life." The *duty* of repentance becomes practicable, when the *grace* is bestowed; that is, when the man is born again.

This grace, however, has its counterfeit, as the expression, "repentance unto life" seems to intimate: there is a repentance not unto life. If a man, under the operation of terror of conscience, break off his sins, and reform his merely outward conduct, and manifest sorrow, and express regret; this is spurious. It is a mere ebullition of selfishness—and a legal repentance: wherein the man does not in reality turn from sin, with loathing, abhorrence, and hatred of it, unto God, with love and delight in holiness. Thus, the criminal at the gallows repents; he laments the sad consequences of his crime; yet could he escape the punishment, he would continue his sinful course.

This suggests an important distinction, as necessary in explanation of these kinds of repentance; viz.—the turning from sin to God is one thing; and the emotions which accompany it, are another. The former has its starting point in the convictions of the intelligence, of which we have spoken as resulting from the enlightening influences of the Holy Spirit. Not only the effects of sin as bringing condemnation upon the soul; but also its moral aspects, as hateful in the sight of God and polluting to the mind and heart, press as a heavy burden upon the conscience. A result of this pressure is a painful apprehension of Divine wrath, commingling with sorrowful feelings, with loathing and revulsion of soul. Now all these feelings, but in infinitely diverse degrees, are dependent on the mental movements. They are not themselves repentance, or the turning of the mind; but accompaniments, less or more intimately associated with the grand movement whereby the soul turns to God.

"Now I rejoice, not that ye were made sorry, but that ye sorrowed to repentance: for ye were made sorry after a godly manner, that ye might receive damage by us in nothing. For godly sorrow worketh repentance to salvation not to be repented of: but the sorrow of the world worketh death:" 2 Cor. vii. 9, 10. Here we have a good illustration of the prophet's remark—"They shall look upon me, whom they have pierced, and they shall mourn for him:" Zech. xii. 10. It is when the soul contemplates the sufferings of Christ, as the consequent of its own sins, that strong feelings overpower it, and sadness and sorrow overwhelm it. The sorrows of saving repentance spring from faith's view of the bleeding cross. And this shows the relation which faith and repentance sustain to each other: the former is the necessary antecedent; for he looks upon him, that is, believes his sufferings were brought about by our sins. "He that cometh to God"—that is, that turneth from sin to God, "must believe that he is, and that he is a rewarder of them that diligently seek him:" Heb. xi. 6. So, repentance unto life is the necessary consequent of saving faith; in the very act of turning, faith is in exercise. And farther, this is the first exercise of the grace of faith. As soon as it is implanted in the soul by the regenerating power of the Spirit, and the eye of faith perceives and appropriates the promises of the gospel, the whole soul turns to God.

It is moreover observable here, that the apostle seems to make the godly sorrow—sorrow toward God, antecedent to and productive of repentance. This emotional state of mind is not only distinguishable from the mental, as a consequent, but as an antecedent and cause—it worketh repentance. On the other hand, the sorrow of the world—sorrow that arises from selfish and worldly apprehensions of danger and loss, has an efficiency, at least an instrumentality, for ruin—it worketh death.

Again, repentance is original and initial, or recurrent and oft repeated. By the former is meant the first movement after the soul is born of God and the principle of faith implanted therein. It is over this mainly that there is joy in heaven; and this it is that is usually understood and referred to in common parlance. But now it is obvious, that the latter is the thing that most abounds; is of daily recurrence; and constitutes a large proportion of the practical duties of the Christian life. As long as Christian men fall into sin—and this will be as long as they are in this world—they will be called upon, yea, and forced, sooner or later, to repent. The case of the Corinthians above cited illustrates this: after their initial repentance, many of them grievously offended, and being reproved severely, were brought up in the face of this duty. So we all fail and come short every day; and every day are called upon to return; and in obeying these calls we find the comfort of our souls.

For, again, repentance is a condition of pardon. By this, however, we do not mean a meritorious basis or foundation to be laid by the sinner, upon which he may claim, as a matter of right, the forgiveness of his sin. The basis of all pardon is laid in the atonement, or satisfaction rendered to Divine justice, by our Redeemer's sufferings and death; on the ground of which, he has a right to claim his people's exemption from the punishment of their sins. To them, therefore, such exemption is pardon and a gratuity; whilst to him, as their surety, it is pure justice. This is the basis and the legal ground of his intercession, for which, "him the Father heareth always." By condition, therefore, is meant simply a required antecedent —that state of mind and feeling must exist, before the pardon comes and the evidence of it can be given to the soul. But, as we have shown, this itself is a gracious state, brought about by the word and Spirit of God; and, of course, to the utter exclusion of human merit. In this restricted sense, regeneration itself, and faith, and initial repentance, as well as repentance recurrent, are conditions of pardon; and indeed, of the entire salvation of the gospel. The conditional graces are bestowed gratuitously, in order that the unconditional glory may be consistent with the justice and holiness of God the giver.

This state of penitential feeling, moreover, is a necessary condition on our part. Without passing into it, pardon would be an unintelligible affair, and unproductive of conscious felicity. But when we look upon Him, whom by our sins we have wounded afresh in the house of his friends, we mourn for him and drop those tears of affection which he will transmute into jewels for the crown of our glory. We see applied anew to our souls, the blood of sprinkling; and feel that our sins are all blotted out, and the light of our Father's countenance shines with renewed radiance upon our souls, then all is reconciliation, peace, and joy. But such felicity is utterly impossible to a soul hardened in impenitence and that refuses to confess its sins before God. On the contrary, "If we confess our sins, he is faithful and just to forgive us our sins, and to cleanse us from all unrighteousness:" 1 John i. 9. Such also was the experience of the Psalmist, "When I kept silence my bones waxed old through my roaring all the day long. * * * I acknowledged my sin unto thee, and mine iniquity have I not hid. I said, I will confess my transgressions unto the Lord, and thou forgavest the iniquity of my sin. * * * Thou shalt compass me about with songs of deliverance:" Ps. xxxii. Thus penitential sorrow is a duty, a means of restoring happiness, and an important branch of sanctification.

Genuine repentance, as it is a necessary consequence and therefore an evidence of regeneration, has, as its necessary sequence, *holy living*, which also is an evidence of a change of heart. This, however, requires time. The tree must grow before it can bear fruit. It is not like the first trees in creation, when "the Lord God made the earth and the heavens, and every plant of the field before it was in the earth, and every herb of the field before it grew." This tree of righteousness springs from the seed of God, develops itself by its own internal activity, then produces its proper fruits, to the praise and glory of the great Husbandman. This fruit-bearing characteristic is all-important as an evidence of regeneration—deferred from chap. xi. By their fruits ye shall know them. When time and opportunity have been adequately afforded, and no fruit follows—or if the vine bears only the grapes of Sodom and the clusters of Gomorrah, it is impossible to believe the tree or the vine to be wholly a right seed—a tree of the Lord's own planting. In the face of this negation, all other evidences shrink away, and are utterly contemned. If the stream is wholly corrupt, no intelligent mind can believe the fountain to be pure. The world, the demon spirits, the man himself, can't believe that he is a renewed man—regenerated—born of God; whilst he continues, as heretofore, to lead an unholy life—"foolish, disobedient, deceived, serving divers lusts and pleasures, living in malice and envy, hateful, and hating one another." Be ye holy, for I am holy.

CHAPTER XV.

SANCTIFICATION COMPARED WITH JUSTIFICATION.

ALTHOUGH we have not yet before us all the parts of that process, by which man is restored to holiness and happiness, the discussion of this comparison may be as profitably introduced here, as at a later period. These two are quite distinct, but intimately related: and it is not practicable, as the reader may have already observed, to keep them altogether from commixture. Let us as a means of this, however, briefly contrast the leading points of difference.

1. Sanctification is a process—a work consisting of an indefinite number of operations, instruments and agencies—yet has it but one efficient Agent.

Justification is an act, done at once and incapable of successive steps. No person can be half justified. The act is either performed, or not performed. Various duties may devolve upon a judge, as he labours through law and evidence towards a decision; just as various instrumentalities prepare for the act of regeneration, whilst itself is one and indivisible; but the decision in favour is one act.

2. The terms, though of exactly similar construction, are yet different in their technical meaning. Sanctification and justification are both Latin words; the former generally means making holy, the latter making just. But technically, the latter means, declaring just, whilst the former is used in its generic sense. Consequently,

3. Sanctification regards moral character and spiritual qualities; justification refers to legal relations. How does a man stand when viewed by the eye of the pure moralist, the holy angels, or the holy God; is the question there. How does he stand in the eye of rigid law—is he guilty, that is, liable to punishment; or is he innocent, and as the law requires? is the question here. Sanctification alters a man's personal qualities. He does not remain the same after that he was before. The very essence of the matter is a radical change for the better, in every moral element. Justification produces no change. When he is pronounced just, he is the same as before sentence passed in his favour; or, on the contrary, (as the terms help to illustrate each other) condemnation, which is the opposite, does not infuse moral turpitude into a man. He is no more corrupt, after the sentence passed against him, than before; it merely declares a change of legal relations; morally, the person is unchanged.

4. The two differ as to their evidences. Sanctification, as already shown, admits different degrees

in its process, and also in the evidences; which are also in kind different from the other. They spring from experience and observation, and are therefore reached by an inductive process. But the evidences of justification are, like the thing itself, received by faith. This grace appropriates Christ's atonement and his righteousness to the person in whom it dwells, and he is thereby made just in the eye of the law; but the evidence of the fact depends upon the grace of faith, which grace falls within the sphere of sanctification by the Spirit; and thus the evidence of the one is largely dependent upon the operations of the other. That a man is justified, he can scarcely, perhaps not at all, know, but through his partial sanctification. By their fruits ye shall know them.

5. More particularly should we notice, that justification is, through the righteousness of Christ, *imputed;* but sanctification is by righteousness or rectitude *inwrought.* The confounding of this distinction gives us the *opus operatum* of the Romanists; one of the radical errors, by which they corrupt the fundamental doctrine of the Bible and substitute self-righteousness in the room of salvation by free grace.

6. In regard to legal merit, if I may so call it, justification has the superiority and the priority over sanctification. The basis or ground-work of justification; viz., the obedience and death of Christ, is the meritorious and procuring cause of

the mission of the Holy Spirit; and, by consequence of the whole work of sanctification; even of that operation of the Spirit, by which the faith that justifies is inwrought in the soul. "It is expedient for you that I go away; for if I go not away, the Comforter will not come unto you; but if I depart, I will send him unto you. And when he is come, he will reprove the world of sin, and of righteousness, and of judgment," &c. John xvi. 7, 8. This same truth is beautifully set forth in the tabernacle service established at Sinai. The sacrifice for the congregation, on the great day of atonement, was slain without, and a portion of the blood was carried into the most holy place, and sprinkled upon the ark of the testimony, to make reconciliation for the sins of the people. This, Paul assures us, represented Christ himself entering, "not into the holy places made with hands, which are the figures of the true, but into heaven itself, now to appear in the presence of God for us:" Heb. ix. 24. On the perfection of his sacrifice the efficacy of his advocacy depends: and thus the atonement secures the mission of the Spirit and the sanctification of the whole redeemed church. No wonder the holy apostle made so much of it, as to constitute or affirm its position as the central truth of the system—"For I determined not to know anything among you, save Jesus Christ and him crucified:" 1 Cor. ii. 2.

9*

CHAPTER XVI.

THE ORDER OF THE GRACES.

CHRONOLOGY is not absolutely excluded from this chapter; yet must it have no controlling influence. Mental states are often so nearly co-existent, as to baffle all attempts at discrimination and collocation in order of time. We must, therefore, rather look to the order of suggestion in our thoughts—the modes or train in which they most naturally occur to us. If a writer closely and successfully note this in his own mind and succeed in passing it over to his paper, he will very probably present them in the way best adapted to enable his readers to conceive and retain them; and this, because the laws of succession in thoughts are few and simple, and common to men.

The reader will remember, that we have excluded conviction of sin from the category of the graces; and that, simply because conviction *per se* is not a grace or a blessing. We think, moreover, that to speak of it so as to produce, or leave in the mind, the vague notion of its being a blessing, exposes to the danger of mistaking conviction for conversion; false confidence for true faith; and, thereby landing the soul in the snares and toils of a dangerous carnal security.

1. The first of the graces is regeneration. When the soul is born of God, it is a new creature. The principle of a holy life is now present. Sanctification is begun. No holy principle or holy action prior to this belongs to it. This is the seed of God, which being within a man, "he cannot sin, (as a habit, that is,) for his seed remaineth in him; and he cannot sin, because he is born of God." 1 John iii. 9. There is, indeed, a slight impropriety, as before intimated, in calling this a grace, for it is not improvable, as contradistinguished from other branches of sanctification. It does not grow, or advance from one degree to another, but is perfected at once. But, as the production of this change from death unto life is a gratuitous and gracious exercise of the Divine energy, it will be productive of no evil, that I can think of, to place regeneration at the head of the graces.

2. Next, not in time, and scarcely in the order of our conceptions; but, as it were, coexistent with the first, is *faith*—the restored principle of holy confidence in God; which, whenever the Divine testimony is presented, sets to its seal that God is true. This grace, implanted in the soul, comes into exercise, the first after it is made alive spiritually. Perhaps I have not, with sufficient explicitness, distinguished between the fixed princi-

ple or abiding law of belief, and the acts of believing. The former is what I mean by the grace of faith and is the fruit of the renewing Spirit; the latter are acts of the mind itself and the works of the new man.. This distinction is important, in order to avoid foisting in the act of believing into the position, in justification, of Christ's righteousness. Those who do this take faith subjectively, which is a mistake; whereas, when faith is counted for righteousness, it is correctly taken objectively. Not the act of believing, but the object on which that act terminates, is accounted for righteousness. The former makes salvation depend upon the sinner's act; the latter builds it upon the Saviour's merits. The one is by works; the other by grace.

3. Saving repentance admits a chronological order. It is a sequence of faith both in time and in the order of our conceptions. The turning of the mind involves an activity of faith; and the measure of strength in the feelings is graduated by the depth of the soul's former iniquities, collated with the height of present spiritual illumination.

4. Love is the crowning grace. "Beloved, let us love one another: for love is of God; and every one that loveth is born of God, and knoweth God. He that loveth not, knoweth not God; for God is love." "Love worketh no ill to his neighbour, therefore love is the fulfilling of the law."—"All the law is fulfilled in one word, Thou shalt love thy neighbour as thyself." Sometimes love to God is

referred to as evidence and reason for love to the brethren : sometimes love to the brethren, as proof of love to God, and, of course, of a change of heart. The reason is obvious, the thing—the principle of communicative goodness, is the same, whether the object upon which it operates be God himself or the children of his love: and in both cases its essential activity goes forth alone with the commencement of its being, in the soul's regeneration. We cannot mark time here: we cannot say the soul after it has believed, and again, after it has repented, comes under the law of love. We cannot conceive a man to be regenerate, a true believer, a sincere penitent, and yet, for a time, devoid of love. This heaven-born principle belongs essentially to the new man ; and, without it, no one can have evidence of his renovated state. Could it lie dormant in the soul, perfectly inactive, it seems impossible the man should know of its existence. But as it is vitally active, not in word only nor in tongue, but in deed and in truth, it cannot lie hid, but must reveal itself.

CHAPTER XVII.

PROGRESSIVE NATURE OF SANCTIFICATION.

WHEREVER there is life, there is action. And wherever there is a life-principle, connected with a material organism, there must be motion. What life is, in either of these spheres, philosophy has struggled hitherto in vain to determine. From its activities we learn the existence of life: and from the peculiar form of its activities, we come to a knowledge of the particular kind of life; whether vegetable, or animal, connected with material substance: or, within the sphere of immaterial substances, whether intellectual or rational; moral or spiritual. Now there seems to be one characteristic common to all life; viz. that its legitimate activities secure and result in its increase and enlargement. Self-aggrandizement is its universal law. Right action—action suitable—accordant with the nature of the life itself, results in its increase. Vital powers are not decreased, but increased by their own proper activities. This law seems to be without any limit, except within the region of material organism. The nature of matter is such, that repulsion and dissolution of its organic forms, seems to be essentially a part of it. Whether the spiritual or psychical body of which Paul speaks, is merely the deliverance of the organic matter of the body, from this repellent and destructive power, does not appear. But it is obvious, that vegetables and animals have a limit set to advancement by their own activities. Otherwise, the onward movement of life seems to be its universal law.

We have here the starting point of the law of progress, which runs through the works of God. Let us briefly look into its operation within the departments of life respectively; beginning with the lowest class.

1. The vegetable kingdom is a vast universe. Its denizens are to us innumerable: even their classification has been but partially accomplished; although the work has occupied mighty intellects from Solomon's to our day. And all these classes, from the microscopic plant, to the cedar of California; and all the individuals of all the classes, have completed their organization under the action of their life; advancing progressively, for so many minutes, or for so many thousand years. Each one has acted out the life which God gave it; performed its functions; reached its limit; given up its life, and returned its material substance to the dust whence it sprang. Now each of these myriads of millions illustrates the principle before us. So the product of the farm. " For the earth bringeth forth

fruit of herself; first the blade, then the ear, after that the full corn in the ear." The parable of the mustard seed illustrates the growing nature of the kingdom of God, by that development and enlargement which results from the activity of the inherent life. Stop this inner activity, and the plant or the cedar dies. Drive its energies to action beyond their natural movement, and you force its premature destruction.

2. Equally simple, yet equally incomprehensible, as to the mode of their action, and equally obvious are the facts within the sphere of animal life. Feeble are its pulsations in the insect that flutters in the sunbeam; powerful are the throes of even its earliest movements in the monsters of the deep, the forest, or the eagle's airy home. But still they are onward and upward: and each reaches, in due time, if unmolested, that measure of perfection assigned to it by its Maker. The unfledged nestling, with naked body and closed eyes, receives its meat from God, through the instinctive laws of its own nature; exerts the feeble powers it has, which every day increase. His bones knit, his muscle and sinew harden and toughen; his feathers spread over him, his wings bear him a little beyond his eyrie; anon, he becomes "a great eagle, with great wings, he comes to Lebanon and takes the highest branch of the cedar"—he descends with fiery eye and with terrible swoop from the summit of Chimborazo, and bears his prey aloft.

3. Passing the bounds of the material world and entering that of immaterial substances, we find the same rule of advancing life. The region of spirits and their attributes are not so easily cognizable. Still we can know something of the laws of mental movement; and we may view them under four aspects—or points of observation; viz., The intelligence, the reason, the moral faculty, and the spiritual.

(1.) The intellectual powers—the mind or soul, viewed as the recipient of knowledge, begins low and ascends to higher regions. How feeble the infantile mind! Has the babe intelligence? Or is it a mere animal, or a mere vegetable, capable of physical action and growth thereby, like a cabbage plant?

Oh with what intense interest such questions come home to the mother's bosom, as she dandles the feeble mortal on the parent knee! And, oh with what feelings her heart swells and her bosom heaves, as she discovers that it sees—oh, yes, it is not born blind—this inlet of knowledge has been bestowed by the all-seeing One. Anon, it startles at the sudden jar of the shutting door. Then it hears, too! thanks to the Hearer of prayer, my babe has another most important inlet of knowledge. A little while, and a little farther expansion and development reveals another power till recently dormant. Yes! oh, yes, in that beautiful eye kindles up the indubitable mark of intelligence; it perceives—it recognizes, it knows me. Thanks to the All-wise, my babe is not an idiot. And thus, as the physical development fits the body for use, as the machinery with which the mind works, the capacity for acquiring knowledge enlarges. Every onward movement becomes the basis of still another and greater advance.

(2.) But let us connect with this the reason. As the mind acquires knowledge, the material for the reasoning faculties increases as the necessity for its use. How the logical faculty expands from the faintest exercises of the comparing power, to the sublimest demonstrations of the astronomer, let the educator testify. He has marked a thousand times, the early essays of the untrained logician; how obscure; how defective and unsatisfactory! But every little gain in knowledge, by inferring truths unknown from those before in possession, becomes a new basis of advance; until at last the infant becomes a giant and grapples with the sublimest demonstrations. Now it is important to remark, that no known limit has been reached, to this intellectual development. It is to us practically interminable. True, our bodily organism, like every other material thing, becomes exhausted and worn out; but this by no means proves a limit to knowledge or the progress of the powers that extend it. The breaking of a bolt or of an axletree does not at all prove that the expansive power of steam has reached its utmost limit. The failing of the mental powers in old men, no more than insanity or idiocy proves a limit to the mind's capacity for enlargement. All these phenomena are resolvable into physical infirmity. Some disorganization of the bodily frame has occurred, so that the mind is clogged and prevented from farther progress.

But now, seeing it is the actual law of the intellect and the reason, to move onward and increase in power, as long as we are acquainted with them here, the question forces itself upon us, Does this law continue beyond the grave? When these trammels of clay, that clog our mental movements, drop off, will our minds cease from their legitimate activity and their growth thereby? Or will they spring forward, with a renewed, a strong, immortal vigour, hitherto unknown? Can it be, that this house of clay is the most suitable abode for the immortal mind, and the best adapted to secure its everlasting expansion?

(3.) Ascending into the higher region of morals, we find ourselves still within the range of progressive advancement. The moral sense itself is under this law. The intellectual part, so to speak, of conscience; that is, its discerning power, is obviously susceptible of great improvement. If a man exercise himself upon questions of moral rectitude —narrowly inspecting his own and other men's conduct, by the light of moral law, he cannot fail of whetting up his faculties to a clearer discrimination between right and wrong; and thereby fitting himself for an easier solution of such questions for the future. On the contrary, a non-user —a total neglect to exercise conscience in this manner, leaves it in all its native feebleness; so that he remains incapable of forming opinions of moral acts, and sinks himself toward the rank and condition of a mere animal.

Necessarily such cultivation or neglect must affect the judging power of conscience. Because, judging is the comparing of ideas, and marking their agreement or difference; and its accuracy will depend upon the correctness of the mind's perceptions of those ideas. The things compared in our processes of moral judgment are the moral law on the one hand, and the conduct of moral agents on the other. The apostle, in 1 John iii. 20, tells us "if our heart"—that is, conscience—"condemn us, God is greater than our heart, and knoweth all things." Our conscience, with the imperfect knowledge we now have, condemns us; much more will God's perfect knowledge insure a more severe condemnation.

The impulsive power of conscience is increased by our careful acquiescence in its decisions, and injured by disregard of its admonitions. Whenever the discriminating and judging activities of the moral sense are passed, its impulsive power is put forth: it commands us to do the right and to avoid the wrong. If we are careful in this matter, our constant and prompt compliance with the dictates and advice of this kind friend will secure his continued and increasing friendship: but woe to him who contemns his voice and rejects his counsel. We are familiar with the hardening process described by Paul, as a searing with a hot iron. 1 Tim. iv. 2: "Speaking lies in hypocrisy, having their conscience seared with a hot iron." How forcibly this expresses the reverse of our doctrine! When reverse operations require, the impulsive power is almost abrogated: whereas, falling in with its decisions and exercising our minds in following up its counsels, there is a constant increase of its power secured and a higher moral stand sustained.

The same remarks are true with regard to the rewarding and punishing power of the moral sense. How rich the consolations of the former; and how terrible the consequences of neglecting the latter! Yet, if we neglect either or both, we lose much on the one hand, and on the other treasure up wrath against the day of wrath, when the never dying worm begins his everlasting torments.

As it is with the moral sense itself, so with the moral virtues which call it forth and coalesce with its activities; they increase under legitimate use. To illustrate in a single case: The love of truth, the requirement of the ninth precept, is undiscovered in early years. It requires time and great attention to generate in the youthful mind the idea of truth and the conception of falsehood: but still more, to waken the moral sense to the perception of its importance and the wrong of its violation. Young children lie or tell falsehoods, without showing any compunction of conscience. But careful management, in a few years, forms their minds to the right conception, and soon secures the active force of the moral sense in its favour. Feeble, indeed, and faint in its movements at first, is the love of truth: but steadfast adherence to it by all around him; the manifestation of strong disapprobation of lying, by those to whom he looks for protection, favour, and kindness, soon strengthen the feeling, and it rises to a law of veracity, and operates as a controlling influence over the whole man.

"Surely they are my people, children that will not lie." And the command is clear, Lie not one to another—All liars shall have their part in the burning lake. And in Ps. xv., "he that speaketh the truth," is laid down as a preparation for ascending into the hill of God. And this habit becomes so established by practice, that it is, as it were, impossible for such men to lie. Yet an opposite course, even after considerable progress has been made, may reverse the whole. Through the power of temptation men are led to falsify, and, succeeding repeatedly in worldly gains by such means, the habit presently swallows up and obliterates all conscientiousness as to truth-telling, and the man is hardened in his iniquity. And thus it is with all the moral habits required by the decalogue. Just as it is with our mere physical powers; they are advanced on their way to perfection by their legitimate exercise.

4. Thus we advance one more step in our ascending series, and find ourselves in the region of spiritual life.

In the close of his second epistle, Peter prescribes obedience to this law: "But grow in grace, and in the knowledge of our Lord and Saviour Jesus Christ." Here is a beautiful allusion to our first illustration—the vegetable kingdom. Trees do grow: graces do grow. Knowledge too, as already seen, has its upward movement. That inimitable allegory in the fifth chapter of Isaiah is based on this law: "My well beloved hath a vineyard in a very fruitful hill: and he fenced it, and gathered out the stones thereof, and planted it with the choicest vines," &c. "For the vineyard of the Lord of hosts is the house of Israel, and the men of Judah his pleasant plant." The vine grows from a small cutting, and advances continually toward perfection. The parable of the mustard seed, and that of the leaven, exemplify the same principle. So the Christian life is a race and a warfare. Ye did run well. Run with patience the race that is set before you. Then shall ye know, if ye follow on to know the Lord. So we hear of babes in Christ, of young men and of old men. Paul, in Heb. v., reproves them for their slow advance. Yet "they go on from strength to strength; every one of them in Zion appeareth before God." "We are changed from glory to glory." So the church is a spiritual house, and of course, has its foundation, its walls and entire superstructure; not created at once, but by successive steps. "And are built upon the foundation of the apostles and prophets, Jesus Christ himself being the chief corner stone; in whom all the building fitly framed together groweth unto a holy temple in the Lord: in whom ye also are builded together for a habitation of God through the Spirit:" Eph. ii. 20–22.

Let these suffice to show, that the law of progress prevails in the domain of the Spirit's work of sanctification.

CHAPTER XVIII.

INSTRUMENTALITIES BY WHICH THE SPIRIT WORKS IN THE PROGRESS OF SANCTIFICATION.

We have already proposed a distinction, in regard to holiness, by the epithets *negative* and *positive:* meaning by negative holiness, the absence of pollution—of corruption—of moral turpitude, without the presence of positive moral purity : and by positive holiness, that presence—purity of actual character—the inbeing of right feelings and habits of upright action. According to this distinction there will be two aspects of the work of making men holy : two processes, easily distinguished from each other : the one is the removal of corrupt lusts—sinful affections out of the soul : the other, the introduction of pure desires, holy affections, actual and positive good spiritual qualities. It is not insisted that these movements are separable, either in time or nature. We need not attempt even to conceive of a soul being freed from all sinful affections, and not yet the abode of pure and holy emotions—a mere. hull of a house, empty, swept and garnished—furnished, though not inhabited. But we think, that both the instrumentalities and the efficiency are different; though intimately related; and, in a degree, commingled. This we shall understand better as we proceed to name some of the leading instruments and occasions of sanctification, as viewed from the negative or from the positive side.

As to the first introduction of holiness into the soul, in the matter of regeneration, we have seen, in Chapter XI. that the moral law is mainly used, but only as an instrument for conviction, expelling the strong man, and emptying the house. For the production of the new life, the Spirit's own direct power is alone efficient.

But now that the seed of God, the life-germ is implanted, it only requires the removal of obstructing hindrances, and the presence of water and warmth, to ensue its expansion and growth. Because this fire and water, this thing symbolized; the Spirit, keeps up the motion and activity of the life, and by this, it grows, like the mustard-seed.

1. The truth is a leading instrument. "Sanctify them through thy truth; thy word is truth." Let us exemplify by reference to the second commandment. Idolatry is a crying sin, and pollutes the whole soul, and disqualifies it for holy duties. This is checked by the truth in the second precept: the habit is condemned; the ruinous consequences of the sin fill the mind with apprehension: conscience

rallies, and this lust of the carnal mind is nailed to the cross. Negatively the soul is advanced in purity. But the effect does not stop in a mere negation—the arrest of a corrupt habit—a positive onward movement also results. The Spirit prompts to the duty of holy reverence for God, and the feelings of the soul, which before went forth after the idol, are now transferred to the proper object of religious awe and reverence. God is erected in place of the idol, and Ephraim cries out, "What have I to do any more with idols?"

Take also an example from the second table. Carnal affections, in violation of the seventh precept, have carried away the heart; and sexual impurity breaks up the peace of families and communities, as almost everywhere in the pagan world. The commandment is sent in power by the Spirit. "Mortify therefore your members which are upon the earth, fornication, uncleanness, inordinate affection," &c. "For if ye live after the flesh, ye shall die; but if ye through the Spirit do mortify the deeds of the body, ye shall live." The soul is made to know that the most secret movement of illicit desire is sinful and perilous: then comes the negation: the flesh is crucified. But again the positive side of sanctification gains. Chastity is cherished, and a life of purity is advanced.

The reader will notice in this twofold operation, the distinctive instrumentalities of the truth respectively, of the law, and of the gospel. To this there is direct reference by the apostle: 2 Cor. iii. 6, where he says, "The letter killeth, but the Spirit giveth life." And again, v. 9, he calls it "The ministration of condemnation." The effect directly of this condemnation of sin in the believer, is to remove obstructions to the practice of holiness —to break up habits of sinning: and so to open the way for positive holiness, in its onward progress by the Holy Spirit's work through gospel truth; encouraging, persuading, and enabling the soul to practise holiness in the fear of God.

2. Another instrumentality is brought to view in the above citation, viz, the living ministry of the word. "Ye are our epistle, written in your hearts. * * * written, not with ink, but with the Spirit of the living God; not in tables of stone, but in fleshly tables of the heart. And such trust have we through Christ to God-ward. Not that we are sufficient of ourselves to think anything as of ourselves; but our sufficiency is of God: who also hath made us able ministers of the New Testament."—Here again we see that the ministry, (important as are the living teachers of the word and exemplifiers of progressive sanctification in their own persons) are nevertheless, only instruments: the Holy Ghost is the Sanctifier. Moreover, as above, the removal of corrupt affections is one thing; and the implantation of positive holiness is another.

Similar are the two forms presented in 1 Peter

ii. 11, 12 : "Dearly beloved, I beseech you, as strangers and pilgrims, abstain from fleshly lusts, which war against the soul; having your conversation honest among the Gentiles : that whereas they speak against you as evil-doers, they may by your good works, which they shall behold, glorify God in the day of visitation." Negation—refusal to gratify, tends to root out positive corruption : and the holy conduct of the saints operates, through the Spirit, positive influence in drawing sinners into the way of holiness.

3. Sufferings, under the chastising hand of a Father, tend in the same direction. The fruit of affliction is to take away sin. "But who may abide the day of his coming? and who shall stand when he appeareth? for he is like a refiner's fire, and like fuller's soap. And he shall sit as a refiner and purifier of silver : and he shall purify the sons of Levi, and purge them as gold and silver, that they may offer unto the Lord an offering in righteousness :" Mal. iii. 2, 3. "I have chosen thee in the furnace of affliction."

This method of purifying the church is prominent throughout her history. "Before I was afflicted I went astray, but now have I kept thy word:" Psalm cxix. 67. Ephraim bemoaned himself thus; "Thou hast chastised me, and I was chastised. * * * Surely after that I was turned, I repented:" Jer. xxxi. 18 : but our Father chastiseth "for our profit, that we might be partakers of his holiness. Now no chastening for the present seemeth to be joyous, but grievous; nevertheless, afterward it yieldeth the peaceable fruit of righteousness unto them which are exercised thereby:" Heb. xii. 10, 11. Plainly, there is nothing in mere suffering calculated to generate kindly feeling toward the person who inflicts it; but the reverse. The executioner is an odious character. The natural and immediate effect of suffering, is grievous, and renders the rod an object of dread. But the association of the pain with the offence that brings on the stroke, calls into action the law of self-love, and thus restrains from its repetition: but it does not generate holy affection: it only operates negatively. It requires another agency and influence to begin or to increase holy action in the soul. The peaceable fruit of righteousness is the effect of another cause: not of the pain; but of the exercise of a spiritual influence, shedding forth love in the heart. So it is even with an earthly parent's chastisement: unless the child is enabled to see love wielding the rod, no beneficial consequence will follow; but hardness, obstinacy, and hate rather.

Under this general head of afflictions, as a means of sanctification in both kinds, are a multitude of things, which it were impossible to detail. The whole book of Job is an exemplification. Destruction of property; death of friends; unreasonableness of counsellors and advisers; alienation of affection in those we love; personal torment under disease and infirmity, &c.; all social evils, such as epidemic, pestilence, war, and famine; and revolutions affecting the whole community and so involving the church; but, above all, persecution. This last is proverbially referred to as a purifier. The blood of the martyrs is the seed of the church; and, indeed, her entire history consists largely of details of sorrows and calamities brought upon her professedly for this end, that she may be prostrated before the Lord, and constrained in dust and ashes to confess and forsake her sins.

How these things operate, it is not difficult to perceive. In the case of riches, for example: if the Christian is in danger of trusting in them, to the neglect of God and his own soul; the Lord, in mercy, gives them wings and they fly away as an eagle towards heaven; and draw his thoughts in that direction. In the case of dear friends coming in between the soul and God. He in mercy takes away the wife, the husband, the son, the daughter, that the idol being removed, God himself may be the only object of supreme regard. Thus, the flesh is crucified, with its lusts and corruptions; hinderances to the onward movement in holiness are removed; and the gracious power of the Spirit carries forward the work from glory to glory.

4. The sacraments, as well as the word, are instruments of growth. Baptism, wherein water is poured as the symbol of the Spirit, sets forth his

purifying influence. Only, however, by reflective activities of the mind, is it to himself and in his own case, an instrument of his own purification. The very thing set forth by it, is "the washing of regeneration, and renewing of the Holy Ghost:" Tit. iii. 5. So that it is not to the subject a means, but as he reflects upon it and keeps up the idea of washing—of spiritual purification; and thus the exhibition of it becomes a standing visible admonition of the necessity of holiness and of the only agency of its production. Every time the eye beholds the water applied in baptism, the beholder is warned of his need of a gracious power to change his heart. Every time he calls up and meditates on its spiritual meaning, he is invited to come and be cleansed; and that whether it be the first act in the new creation of the soul; or subsequent movements of the same power in the progress of holiness.

Moreover, in the case of the baptized, as a seal of the covenant, it is a standing memorial of their obligations to lead a holy life, to the glory of God and their own everlasting welfare; and of the sealed promise on the part of God, to minister the spiritual graces necessary to meet these covenant obligations.

But it is the sacred supper, that chiefly symbolizes the means of growth in holiness. Herein the exhibition of bread and wine separately, holds up the cross before our eyes. The only sacrifice, that can take away sin, as to its guilt, and secure the ultimate removal also of its pollution, is kept before us, and our faith is constrained to dwell upon it, and appropriate it to ourselves; before whose eyes Jesus Christ is evidently set forth crucified. As we appropriate the bread and the wine, the symbols of his body and blood, we say, each for himself, " He loved me and gave himself for me." When we do this in remembrance of him, we bring him up vividly before our own minds. We hear his agonizing prayer—the only prayer of his, to which, in appearance, the Father turned a deaf ear. —" Father, if it be possible, let this cup pass from me,"—his dying shriek pierces our hearts, and as we look upon him, we mourn for him and weep over those sins that pierced the Lord of glory. We feel that he is present according to his promise. His matchless—wondrous love swells in our bosom, and we know it is his Spirit that kindles up afresh this flame that can never die. At the banquet of wine, we open our hearts and make large requests for renewing grace; seal anew the covenant of life, and pledge our souls and all that is within us, that, in all coming time, and by his grace, in all eternity, we will be his. Thus we are carried back to the very foundation of our hope; for here is the work which secures the mission of the Spirit, and he by this strengthens our faith and refreshes our souls, and invigorates every power for renewed activity and energy.

CHAPTER XIX.

TEMPTATION AND PRAYER—MEANS OF GROWTH.

These cannot well be classed with the mere *instruments* used by the Spirit; and yet they are important means which he does use or overrule for the purification of his church. I put temptation before, for the reason, that prayer is a means of deliverance. "Watch and pray that ye enter not into temptation." "Count it all joy when ye fall into divers temptations." Hence it is evident, that the word is used in an evil sense; and also in a good sense. Temptation is an evil to be guarded against; it is a good to be rejoiced over. We infer that, by itself, temptation is indifferent—neither good nor bad necessarily; but depending for its character upon the circumstances of each case; and especially on the tendency and design of the tempter. The general meaning is *trial*—putting a person to some test, which will reveal his temper, disposition, inclination. It implies uncertainty—doubt as to whether the person is as he professes or appears to be. The instances, however, of its application in a good sense are few; Scripture usage is chiefly in an ill sense. Of the former we have, Gen. xxii. 1, "God did *tempt* Abraham;" and Jas. i. 2, cited above; and there is not a third; so that it may be assumed, that temptation in Scripture means an effort to draw aside from the path of duty by placing motives to evil before the mind. Thus the Israelites tempted God; Satan tempted our Saviour in the wilderness, by endeavouring to induce him to use unlawful means for personal aggrandizement. "Let no man say when he is tempted, I am tempted of God; for God cannot be tempted with evil, neither tempteth he any man." He tempted Abraham, it is true, but not for the purpose and design of inducing him to act sinfully. It was in order to draw forth and manifest his faithfulness and integrity. And the other case calls for all joy, not because of the "divers temptations" in themselves, but rather for the results when believers have resisted them. In this light it is, that temptation is used by the Spirit as a means and occasion for advancing the soul in holiness. "For there hath no temptation taken you —(says Paul to the Corinthians, i. 10, 13—) but such as is common to man; but God is faithful, who will not suffer you to be tempted above that ye are able; but will with the temptation also make a way to escape, that ye may be able to bear it." Hence the direction in prayer—"Lead us not into temptation, but deliver us from evil;" perhaps better "from the evil one." As Christ was delivered from the tempter, so will he ensure deliverance to all his people; and as with himself and his friend Abraham, so shall it be with all the faithful. Not only shall their adversaries be foiled; but their graces shall shine forth with increased brilliancy and glory. Through the furnace of affliction shall they walk unharmed and shall come forth without the smell of fire upon their garments. Bound they may be, when they are thrown in, but their bonds shall be consumed and they shall walk loose, because beside them " the form of the fourth is like the Son of God." The lions' mouths are shut, because the Angel Redecmer has unfolded the glory of his own Divine presence in their den, and they can go no farther than he permits. The Holy Ghost inhabits his temple, therefore the spirits of pollution cannot there dwell.

> "Trials make the promise sweet,
> Trials give new life to prayer;
> Trials bring me to his feet,
> Lay me low, and keep me there."

The storms that rock the sapling, and bow its head almost to the earth, send its roots the deeper into the soil; and prepare the mighty oak or the majestic cedar to brave the tempests of a thousand years. Great temptations triumphed over make great Christians. It may be well for a moment to ask how temptations may be resisted and good be deduced from the evil: and no better lesson can be found, than the Master's example and his command by his servant, James iv. 7, " Resist the devil, and he will flee from you. Draw nigh to God, and he will draw nigh to you. Cleanse your hands, ye sinners; and purify your hearts, ye double-minded." The Holy Spirit within resists the unholy spirit, and keeps him out; and the consequence is, the hands are cleansed and the heart is purified.

But there is an instrumentality to be used. "Put on the whole armour of God, that ye may be able to stand against the wiles of the devil. * * * Stand therefore, having your loins girt about with truth; and having on the breastplate of righteousness: and your feet shod with the preparation of the gospel of peace: above all taking the shield of faith, wherewith ye shall be able to quench all the fiery darts of the wicked. And take the helmet of salvation, and the sword of the Spirit, which is the word of God: praying always with all prayer, and supplication in the Spirit:"—Eph. vi. 14, &c. Most of these implements have been already considered. The sword in the Saviour's hands was very effective in repelling the arch-fiend: and we have therein a strong argument in favour of a similar application. By these weapons, wisely used, we must gain the victory.

Prayer, as a religious exercise, " is the offering up of our desires to God."—" Deliver us from the evil one." Prayer is not a duty peculiar to Christians. It is a duty under the law of nature

—it is a necessary attribute of dependent rational existence. All intelligent beings do pray—do send forth their desires—express their wants: some, to the true God through Jesus, the Mediator, and by the aids of the Holy Spirit: some, as the heathen, to false gods—Jupiter, Bacchus, Ashtaroth or Venus; or, as the Romans now, to the Virgin Mary, the saints, Peter, Paul, &c. Some pray to Fortune, an old Roman goddess, yet ardently worshipped.

Prayer is a means, pointed out by the law of nature, as well as by the Scriptures, for obtaining a supply of our wants. It is placed here at the close of the heavenly panoply, doubtless for the reason, that it calls forth those influences which give energy and efficiency to all the rest. "Praying always with all prayer and supplication *in* the Spirit"—*by* the Spirit, I prefer. "Likewise the Spirit also helpeth our infirmities: for we know not what we should pray for as we ought: but the Spirit itself maketh intercession for us with groanings which cannot be uttered." Rom. viii. 26, &c. Some people seem to think themselves capable of going beyond the Spirit, by showing that their groanings can be uttered. But it appears plain, that the inhabiting Spirit goes beyond our very thoughts, and procures for us blessings above our knowledge: working in us both to will and to do of his good pleasure. Pray without ceasing—men ought always to pray and not to faint. An habitual feeling of want tends to keep down the pride of the heart, and so to mortify the flesh with its lusts and corruptions. The new man can no more live without praying, than the old carnal man can live without breathing. Beautifully has it been said, prayer is the breath of the new man. As breathing keeps up the life of the body, and is indispensable, not only to its growth, but to the continuity of its being; so prayer is indispensable to the being and advancement of our spiritual life. Nor need the *modus operandi* give us any trouble. Wherein lies the efficacy of prayer? How doth it expand the powers of the renewed heart? I answer, wherein lies the efficacy of natural breath? How doth the heaving of the bosom continue and increase my physical energies, and extend my life? Should all men refuse to breathe until they can understand all these modes of influence, the race would soon die out, and the earth be left a desolation. Oh no: man is not omniscient: let him not attempt to limit God. If I could know nothing at all, of the mode in which prayer is efficacious, this I do know; that God commands all 'men everywhere to pray without ceasing.

CHAPTER XX.

THE FRUIT OF THE SPIRIT.

If we live in the Spirit let us also walk in the Spirit. This is a result of his inhabitation. He dwelleth in us in order that we abound in good works. Some of these, connected with external instrumentalities, have passed under review: others, not a few, are not so connected: but are produced by his independent action. These we may now consider under the classification furnished in Gal. v. 22, 23: "The fruit of the Spirit is love, joy, peace, long-suffering, gentleness, goodness, faith, meekness, temperance." Two of these have already been before us, yet we shall, bearing very lightly upon those two, make a few remarks upon this catalogue of nine topics.

1. Love is the principle of communicative goodness. It is essentially active, always aiming to do good to the person who is the object of it. It is the universal principle of moral excellence; has its origin in God; was lost in the first sin, and is restored only when the soul is renewed after the image of him that created it.

2. Joy is an elevation or lifting up of the soul; an emotional state of mind, of a very pleasing character; resulting from an apprehension of some great good, either in possession or prospect. A few instances will illustrate. Matt. xxv. 21: "Well done, thou good and faithful servant—enter thou into the *joy* of thy lord." Luke vi.: "Rejoice ye in that day, and leap for joy." Strong feeling is here displayed, because of great benefits in view, productive of great happiness. The state of feeling in heaven, upon the reception of the news of sinners repenting on earth, is expressed by this word, Luke xv. 7, 10. When the news were received that the Gentiles had embraced the gospel, "the disciples were filled with joy and with the Holy Ghost." Acts xiii. 52. And thus everywhere: joy is a strong and glad emotion resulting from the obtaining of some great benefit. This benefit is the glorious hope of the soul, that it hath found the Messias; and it is called a fruit of the Spirit, because he produces the change from death unto life; and also the evidence of the change.

3. *Peace* is the third fruit. Being justified by faith, we have peace with God. By nature we are enemies; the carnal mind is enmity against God. Now to be at enmity and war with a power vastly beyond our own, is a painful and distressing condition: and to stand in that relation with the Almighty, is fearful indeed. But God is angry with the wicked every day, and his anger burns with in-

tense fierceness, and must in the end devour his adversaries. Oh how desirable then to be restored to peace! But this peace is purchased by the death of our Blessed Lord. He is our Peace. How then is it a fruit of the Spirit? Because, though the price has been paid, yet actual peace on our part does not exist, until the heart is changed, the enmity slain, and reconciliation in fact restored. This is the work of the Spirit, and hence it is classed as here.

We ought however to remark, that it is not only peace with God, but also with all holy beings : just as the first fruit extends its blessed influence, as well to the children of God, as to their Father in heaven. This peace pervades the entire family of holy intelligences—a peace, therefore, that passeth understanding.

4. *Long-suffering* is a modification of love and peace. It is spoken of God, Rom. ii. 4, and ix. 22: " Or despisest thou the riches of his goodness, and forbearance, and long-suffering."—" God endured with much *long-suffering* the vessels of wrath fitted to destruction." In Eph. iv. 2, it is applied to men—" With long-suffering, forbearing one another in love." Patient endurance—bearing long—and not soon angry at sinners, out of a feeling of friendship and love, seems to be the general idea. And that such should be the consequence of the love of God and the peace which passeth all understanding shed abroad in the heart, by the Spirit, is most

reasonable to expect. Hence this is accounted in the number of these gracious fruits.

5. *Gentleness*, suavity, amiability, freedom from stiff and surly temper. It is very difficult to mark the boundaries between this and the 8th fruit, *meekness*—unassuming mildness, softness of temperament. They combine and in fact commingle; but express qualities greatly productive of Christian harmony and promotive of happy intercourse in society.

6. The sixth fruit, in order, we must treat in the same way. We have so few words in our language expressive of the various shades of moral emotions, that we can find no one to mark the precise phase of the emotional states. *Goodness* is perhaps the most suitable, though evidently very general. This presents a feeling very nearly allied to the first; it leads toward such actions as conduce to the happiness of all around.

7. The seventh in order is *faith*, used here in the sense of *confidence:* freedom from a spirit of distrust and jealousy: a moral virtue, rather than the great leading grace, of which we have already spoken.

9. *Temperance*, continence, self-control. This may have reference to what is now technically called "temperance." Rather, however, it refers to control over the sexual feeling. At least it is much broader than recent custom has allowed. Peter places it in his catalogue of virtues thus, 2 Pet. i. 5, 6 : " And besides this, giving all dili-

gence, add to your faith virtue, and to virtue, knowledge; and to knowledge, temperance; and to temperance, patience; and to patience, godliness." Paul (Titus i. 8, 22,) enjoins on bishops and aged men to be temperate: and, 1 Cor. ix. 25, tells us, that "every man that striveth for the mastery—(such as the athletæ in the Grecian games)—is temperate in all things."

Such are among the beneficial consequences of this work of the Spirit. In perfecting the moral virtues and the Christian graces, he leads the minds and hearts of the saints onward by successful steps, perfecting holiness in the fear of the Lord. "The path of the just is as the shining light, that shineth more and more unto the perfect day:" Proverbs iv. 18.

CHAPTER XXI.

SANCTIFICATION IMPERFECT—OBJECTION.

WHATEVER may be properly called a process or progressive work, must, by the very necessities of its own nature, be imperfect, at some point; or, indeed, at an indefinite number of points in the line of its progress. The point at which the movement stops; and when there is no more corrupt affection to be removed; or at which the soul is never, henceforth, to acquire any increment of holy feeling, of heavenly love, its sanctification may be accounted perfect; although it is plain, that the word perfect is used there in an imperfect sense. It is altogether undeniable, that the great body of Christians have felt and do feel upon themselves a burden of sinful desires. And this is especially so with such as are most eminent for good works. " Brethren, I count not myself to have apprehended: but this one thing I do, forgetting those things that are behind, and reaching forth to those things which are before, I press toward the mark, for the prize of the high calling of God in Christ Jesus;" Phil. iii. 12, &c. " For I know that in me (that is in my flesh) dwelleth no good thing: for to will is present with me; but how to perform that which is good, I find not. * * * But I see another law in my members, warring against the law of my mind, and bringing me into captivity to the law of sin which is in my members:" Rom. vii. 18, 23. "For the flesh lusteth against the spirit, and the spirit against the flesh; and these are contrary, the one to the other; so that ye cannot do the things that ye would:" Gal. v. 17. Hundreds of texts might be adduced containing this humble and self-abasing confession. The apostle John indeed asserts, "He that committeth sin is of the devil"—belongs to the family of Satan. But then, the drift of the context shows, that he speaks of the habitual course of action: the man whose business is to commit sin—who is constantly seeking the gratification of fleshly lusts, is not born of God. On the contrary, a little before, i. 8: "If we say we have no sin, we deceive ourselves, and the truth is not in us. * * * If we say, that we have not sinned, we make him [God] a liar, and his word is not in us." "For there is not a just man upon earth, that doeth good and sinneth not:" Eccl. vii. 20. To me, the idea is a paradox inconceivable, of a human being—for we cannot say, a sinner—on his knees in the closet, duly exercising faith in Jesus Christ, and yet not confessing his personal sins and short-comings, and beseeching his Father, who seeth in secret, to forgive him, for his dear Son's sake. Such a closet occupied by such a Christian, such a Father's omniscient eye hath surely never beheld. Oh no; when Christians fall down in secret or even in social prayer, their speculations about sinless perfection are all and instantly a nullity, and they seek forgiveness; and moreover, they cry for more grace, that they may become more holy and active in fruit-bearing to the glory of God. These two constitute the sum of Christian religious experience, viz., the conflict—the war against "sin that dwelleth in us;" and the pressing on in the ways of holy obedience, "My soul followeth hard after thee."

Now, from this conscious imperfection of the Divine life within him, the true Christian often meets with a practical difficulty, so great at times as to raise doubts, painful and distressing, as to the fact of his own conversion. As in the conflict between Saul and David—which is a real, historical allegory, illustrative of this very point—he is so sorely pressed, that he says "in his heart, I shall now perish one day by the hand of Saul:" 1 Sam. xxvii. 1. But these seasons of doubt pass away; "And there was long war between the house of Saul and the house of David; but David waxed stronger and stronger, and the house of Saul waxed weaker and weaker:" 2 Sam. iii. 1. So shall it be in the long war against sin that dwelleth in us; the victory is sure in the end, and this is the victory that overcometh the world, even our faith. It may be well for us, however, to inquire how it comes, that to the Christian himself he often appears to be retrograding, or at least to be gaining almost nothing in the life of holiness; whilst to other Christians, and even to the world, he seems to become every day more like his divine Master. The solution is this. The longer and the more steadfastly he gazes upon the cross and the face of his divine Lord, the holier he appears, and thus the Christian's standard rises faster than he himself rises; he, like Moses, having no glass in which to behold himself, remains unconscious of the change upon himself. Others can see the shining of his face, even to the dazzling of their eyes; whilst the brightness of the Saviour's glory absorbs his vision, and he conceives himself to be relatively, as it were, falling back. The stars disappear when the sun rises. When the day-star of Jacob arises, the soul is able to survey it distinctly and to admire its twinkling beauties; but when the Sun of righteousness approximates the zenith and bursts in upon it with all his effulgence, all mere reflections of its light are lost in the overwhelming blaze of his glory.

CHAPTER XXII.

SANCTIFICATION COMPLETED, NEGATIVELY—REMARKS ON IDENTITY.

THE question closes in upon us: must this imperfection continue evermore? Is this warfare to last for ever? In this race, is the goal never to be reached? Oh! when, if "by one offering he hath perfected for ever them that are sanctified:" Heb. x. 14,—oh when shall it be? We answer, as to the negative side of sanctification, at death; as to the positive, in eternity; that is, never.

Sanctification, negatively considered, is perfected at death. "The souls of believers are, at their death, made perfect in holiness, and do immediately pass into glory." This is a necessary consequence of the doctrine, that without holiness no man shall see the Lord. Heaven is everywhere in Scripture accounted a holy place and state: "No unclean person hath any inheritance in the kingdom of Christ and of God:" Eph. v. 5. And Gal. v. 19 –21: "Now the works of the flesh are manifest, which are these, adultery, fornication, uncleanness, &c.; of which I tell you before, as I have also told you in time past, that they which do such things shall not inherit the kingdom of God." "Depart from me, ye cursed, I never knew you." "God is angry with the wicked every day." And all the proofs for the necessity of regeneration, are also proofs that this purifying process must be perfected before the soul can dwell with God in heaven.

Take along with this the fact, that whenever the soul is released from the body it is present with the Lord. Reject the pagan notion of purgatory; and the Priestleyan dream of an entirely unconscious sleep from death to the resurrection; and you force us upon the conclusion, that the war against fleshly lusts ceases, the goal of negative holiness is reached; all actual pollution is entirely done away, at death. The last of the Canaanites is driven out of the land. The old man, who was nailed on the cross, in the day when thorough conviction entered the soul, and who has been dying gradually, but surely, now heaves his last sigh and expires.

Positive sanctification is an endless process. We have already seen—Chap. XVII., that the law of progress characterizes the whole department of life—the vegetable and the animal kingdoms; the intellectual and rational; the moral and spiritual. Life connected with material organism has its limits under this law; because of the repulsive and destructive nature of material substance. But life in the intelligence and the reason is an ever onward movement; knowledge is always increasing, and the reasoning powers expand by their own activity, throughout the whole range of our acquaintance with them, over the whole field of our observation. The moral sense improves continually by its legitimate action; and the moral virtues increase their power in the same way.

So also, within the region of spiritual life, growth in grace is the law, retardation or retrogression, real or apparent, is the exception. External violence or an unfavourable season, excessive drought or blight, may cause a temporary pause; but the current of life is not broken up: still its movement is onward—the tree grows.

Here, then, we meet the most interesting question. Does the soul in any or all of these four aspects—intellectual, rational, moral, or spiritual, cease its growth at death? Or does the law of progress pass with it beyond the grave? Our response is, that, All the analogies of God's living creations return a negative to the former; and an affirmative answer to the latter. They all go to shut us up to the belief of a progression without end in all these four respects. Bishop Butler, in his "immortal Analogy," has settled this question; and we suppose it is one of the rare cases that will stay settled. He has demonstrated, by their own most clear and energetic force, that there is no reason whatever to believe that any of our living powers are extinguished and lost for ever. To the high argument in his first chapter we refer the reader. Our brief pages will not admit of its transfer, and its solidity renders it incompressible. To attempt an epitome were presumption. Yet, whilst the reader is studying it, we must be indulged in a few remarks, adapted to open up the way; and to enable us to present the argument for an endless progression in the future world.

1. Identity, or sameness of being, is assumed in the preceding discussion on progress. Without this, the very idea of onward movement in life is not conceivable. Continuity of existence is the indispensable basis of progress. What then is identity?

(1) This question is inapplicable to mere dead matter, until you descend to the first element—the atom—the indivisible particle. For, obviously, all combinations of material particles are fortuitous and for ever undergoing changes. Therefore,

(2) When we speak of sameness in reference to masses of matter, we always have reference to some kind of agglomeration, arrangement, or organization; as a carriage, a ship, a tree, an animal, a man. And in all these, absolute sameness of material particles is never meant to be affirmed. On the contrary, there is a constant changing of atoms. The carriage loses at every turn of its wheels. The ship loses a sail, a rope, a spar, a mast, a plank, a rib, from day to day; and these

are replaced as need requires, until nearly every several part of the vessel is new; and yet it is the same identical vessel still. So, the tree—this towering cedar, is the same that fifteen centuries ago had well nigh perished under the hoof of the passing buffalo; although, meanwhile, it has lost in leaves and branches ten thousand times its original bulk. So, of the buffalo himself; this huge beast is the same animal which a few years since a man might take up and carry under his arm. So of the man himself; he is the same animal that nursing mother dandled on her knee. Therefore,

(3) Within the sphere of dead matter, identity consists not in absolute sameness of particles; but in sameness of form, structure and name, which gives unity of idea. In the lower forms of living things, identity consists in unity and sameness of the life-principle: the life of the seedling is absolutely the same as that of the towering cedar. So the animal—brute and human—as to its material part is similar, in its perpetual changes, to the tree or the ship: but its life is the same identical principle that actuated its infantile movements.

2. Whilst our animal part is subject to the laws common to all of that class, our soul is altogether different. The human animal, whilst it is united with an intelligent, rational spirit, constitutes really no essential part of the human personality. The material substance, with which our spirit is here connected, is no part of ourselves. If I shave or

cut off my hair; if blood is drawn from my veins or my limbs are amputated, my identity is no more affected than is that of a tree when autumn strips off its leaves. *I myself*—this intelligent, conscious, reasoning, feeling, conscientious, active being, am the same identical person that I was before this bodily organization was reduced by hunger, amputation, disease, to the twentieth part of its former bulk. My hearing fails, my eyes go out, and I am left in darkness; my sense of taste and of smell are nearly extinct, and feeling is paralyzed; still I am the same man. It is not the eye that sees, any more than the optic glass: this glass stands in the same precise relation to the operation of vision, as does the eye-ball. Equally and alike, the living organ and the dead, are merely instruments with which the mind or soul sees. And so it is with all the other senses. By a mysterious and hitherto inscrutable connection, the thinking being, myself, uses certain parts of this nervous structure as instruments of perception; but the mode of that connection and use is utterly unknown to us. The senses are indeed inlets of knowledge to the soul within; but when knowledge is let in, even in small quantity, the mind acts independently on the body. This is evident from two facts: first, where the senses fail, or are originally deficient, as in the case of Julia Brace, the mind does not lose its power of action. And secondly, It is known to every one who thinks at all, that his processes of reasoning are carried on best when the bodily organs of sensation are most thoroughly shut up. On the contrary, noise, odours, taste, smell, touch —any excitation of the nervous system by them arrests the operations of thinking and creates confusion in the mind.

3. Identity consists of continued existence through successive portions of time; and it is dependent on the Divine Power. Our knowledge of it is obtained from present consciousness of our present activity, combined with the remembrance of past consciousness. If the power of memory had no existence, we could have no knowledge of our personal identity. I could not know that I am the same person, who wrote Chapter XX. yesterday for I could have no knowledge of past time and its contents. Now, memory is not a bodily organ, but a mental power. Lord Nelson was still the glory of England's navy, after half his body was cut away. His personal identity was not affected, nor did he lose half his memory. General Howard is more of a man to-day and has more power of memory, than most men who have two arms and two legs. Let us now return to the question of eternal progression in holiness.

CHAPTER XXIII.

THE LAW OF PROGRESS PASSES BEYOND THE GRAVE —SANCTIFICATION POSITIVE—AN ETERNAL ONWARD MOVEMENT.

THERE being no reason whatever to believe, that we lose, at the death of the body, any one of our living powers; and the fact being indubitable, that they are all governed by the law of progress, so far as we have knowledge of them, and so far as they are not checked and restrained by their present connection with these clogs of clay; and it being a law of logic which is eternal, and also accordant with the common sense of all mankind, that the uniform course of events heretofore will continue to be the course of events hereafter; we are shut up to the conviction, that these living powers will continue to exist, after they drop the last fragmentary clog of clay: and will continue to act under the same law of onward and upward for ever. If any man question this doctrine, let him adduce his proof. Possession is nine points of the law. If you dispute my title, bring your ejectment and try its strength: the burden of proof lies upon you.

There is, as Butler has shown, no other reason, apart from revelation, for belief in any future course of events, but our knowledge of the past course—that is, the established laws of nature, or order of things which God has ordained, will and must continue, until he sees proper to alter them. The existence of such laws—that is, of uniform antecedence and consequence, is the sole foundation of all inductive reasoning and the sciences which it generates. Root up this foundation, and the entire glorious structures of the modern experimental philosophy tumble into ruins and become a vast chaotic mass.

Here then we take our stand. On the continuance of this law of progress in the human spirit, as on Pisgah's top, we place our feet, and look over the Jordan into the promised land. If this doctrine be not true, then it would follow, that,

1. Reasoning from what has been the order of nature, to what will be, is fallacious. The uniform course of the soul of man—the intelligence, the reason, the moral man and the spiritual—hitherto has been onward and upward, but now, that it is freed from clogs of clay, it stops and advances toward perfection no more.

2. The entire analogies of God's living creations —yea, of his works universal, are broken up. From the first movement upon the chaotic mass, toward consummating the work of creation, arrangement, order, advancement, onward and upward, are the

law. But now, at the very point where reason expects not only the continuance, but a greatly accelerated velocity in the heaven-ward movement, this philosophy commands a halt. Who believes it?

3. If sanctification—growth in all the holy affections—does not continue after death, then was Paul in great error, when he said, "I have a desire to depart and to be with Christ, which is far better;" Phil. i. 23; for he knew and gloried in the fact that he was advancing in holiness, by fighting the good fight and pressing on toward the goal of victory. This is the law of his being here, but on the hypothesis we combat, this progress ceases at death. Obviously then, he had better remain in this condition of perpetual advancement, than to pass into a state where there is no farther growth toward the perfection of God.

4. This doctrine nullifies the universal law of morality, that holy action must be rewarded. For if there is to be no increase in holiness after death —if the soul is to remain stationary, then, either there are no holy activities, or they go unrewarded. But if the doctrine of our second and third chapters is true, and increase in happiness is a moral consequence of holy action unavoidable in the Divine government, then are we thrown back upon the glorious and soul-stirring conclusion, that everlasting progress in holiness, and consequently in happiness, is the law of God's redeemed.

5. Nor let it be supposed on the other extreme,

that this law is inoperative in the previous stages of the divine life in the soul. On the contrary, we hold that, from the new birth onward, all the activities of the new creature are rewarded in the strictest sense. The parable of the talents illustrates this: and also, the promise of grace to the humble: the cup of cold water is rewarded: out "of his fulness have all we received, and grace for grace"—one measure of grace faithfully improved ensures another—and James iv. 6, says, " But he giveth more grace, wherefore he saith, God resisteth the proud, but giveth grace unto the humble." In short, the Bible overflows with this idea, of God's giving grace and then rewarding the activities of it by more enlarged communications of the same. These promises are, however, to the faithful, the believing, the regenerate, the holy. Not to those who have no grace at all is the command to grow in grace given, and the promise of more. And here is a lamentable mistake into which unregenerate men often fall. They transmute the promises addressed to believers into a law of works, and make their own doings, their "dead works," Heb. ix. 14, a condition of salvation. How unphilosophical! how absurd, to suppose that the tree can grow when it has no life! "First make the tree good and his fruit good." "Do men gather grapes off thorns or figs off thistles?"

With this, (which is in fact the foundation principle of inductive science) we have a cause, and may look for its effect. This seed of God remaining in him—this "anointing which ye have received of him abiding in you, you need not that any man teach you: but as the same anointing teacheth you of all things, and is truth, and is no lie, and even as it hath taught you, ye *shall abide* in him:" 1 John iii. 27, and iv. 9. "He that believeth on the Son hath everlasting life."—How is it everlasting, if it may and shall cease to-morrow?— "He that hath begun a good work in you, will perform it unto the day of Jesus Christ:" Phil. i. 6. "And I give unto them eternal life; and they shall never perish, neither shall any pluck them out of my hand:" John x. 28, 29. The Scriptures abundantly teach the perseverance of the saints in grace and holiness. Not, you will observe, the perseverance in grace of the ungodly, the unregenerate, the unholy; but of the saints, the believing, the regenerate. Nor is their perseverance the effect of their merely human resolve and firm determination, but of the Divine Spirit's inhabitation and "working in them to will and to do of his good pleasure." This one doctrine of endless progression in holiness, beginning with regeneration and advancing under the culture of the Spirit that dwelleth in us, involves the perseverance of the saints; and at the same time gives us a beautiful philosophical explanation of the whole matter.

Seizing the prime element of moral government; viz., that upright, holy action must be rewarded;

and providing the germ of holy life in the new birth; and the growth of it by the dews of heavenly grace, it forces us along the glorious ascent. The first pulsations of spiritual life flow forth toward God in acts of faith, and repentance, and love, and new obedience; and these holy acts require and receive their reward, in additional strength and grace, and love shed abroad in the heart by the indwelling Spirit. Then the soul, with this increment of the new life-power, braces itself up for increased activity in all the duties of holy living; and pours forth its gratitude and embodies its more ardent love in doing good to man and giving glory to God. Again, these increased activities call forth increased rewards; and thus the Christian's life is a fire that feeds itself: by the necessities of the new nature which God has given and by the laws of the glorious Giver, it must be onward and upward.

And for proof of this, we appeal to the experience of regenerate sinners, the world over. Such is their testimony in all ages and to the end of this pilgrim life. For,

> "This life's a dream, an empty show;
> But the bright world to which I go,
> Hath joys substantial and sincere;
> When shall I wake and find me there?
> O glorious hour! O blest abode!
> I shall be near and like my God,
> And flesh and sin no more control
> The sacred pleasures of the soul."

That the onward movement should here receive no new impulse, is not conceivable. The controlling influence of flesh and sin being abolished at death, the freed spirit bounds forward and upward with an alacrity and an energy utterly inconceivable by us in this present state. "Eye hath not seen, nor ear heard, neither have entered into the heart of man, the things which God hath prepared for them that love him:" 1 Cor. ii. 9. "Beloved, now are we the sons of God, and it doth not yet appear what we shall be; but we know that, when he shall appear, we shall be like him; for we shall see him as he is:" 1 John iii. 2. With more than angelic wing the soul takes its upward flight. Higher and yet higher it soars aloft. Passing unredeemed angels in its glorious ascent, it takes its position in the grand choir—that immense multitude which no man can number. These all "arrayed in that fine linen which is the righteousness of the saints:" Rev. xix. 8, and holding in their hands their golden harps, they strike notes of praise to redeeming love, in strains so lofty and grand that angels might long to equal. Then, according to the law of their being and of their God, they receive an addition to their holiness, and grace, and power to strike a still higher strain; and thus, it is a fire that feeds itself; *onward and upward;* ONWARD AND UPWARD for ever toward the perfection of God. And this, dear reader, is what I meant, by asserting, that your sanctification, if indeed it be begun, will never, on the positive side, be finished—but will run away into eternity. Oh! how important then for you and for me, to look well to the matter, and see that there be no "if indeed it be begun" in our case—that all doubt be removed from the question of our being born again!

CHAPTER XXIV.

THE JUDGMENT—A CONFIRMATION IN HOLINESS AND BLISS; NOT AN END OF MORAL GOVERNMENT.

The resurrection of our bodies in incorruption—spiritual bodies; their re-union with our souls and reconstruction of our human personality; their passing under the judgment of our glorified Redeemer and thereby receiving confirmation in eternal felicity—"Come, ye blessed of my Father, inherit the kingdom prepared for you from the foundation of the world:" Matt. xxv. 34. All these seem properly to belong to the work of sanctification; except judgment, which, however, necessarily intervenes. In some respects it had been as well to have treated them sooner; but in others, perhaps it is better to close with them.

"Why should it be thought a thing incredible with you, that God should raise the dead?" Acts xxvi. 8. Thus Paul insinuates, that even the heathen ought, by the light of reason and the dim traditions of the ancient revelations, to have arrived at belief in a resurrection. Reason and tradition lead to the belief that justice in some degree is a Divine attribute. But that full and perfect justice is administered here, in this world, is manifestly not true. Wicked men prosper, live happy, as they count happiness, oppress the poor and the upright; and die without due punishment. David, in Psalm lxxiii., discusses this subject. "For I was envious at the foolish, when I saw the prosperity of the wicked. For there are no bands in their death, but their strength is firm. They are not troubled as other men; neither are they plagued like other men. * * * When I thought to know this, it was too painful for me; until I went into the sanctuary of God; then I understood their end." He was almost ready to conclude, there is no just God presiding over the world. But when he went into the sanctuary— when he consulted the Divine teaching, and considered the end or final state of the ungodly, his doubts vanished, his faith triumphed over his cogitations—"Thou shalt guide me with thy counsel, and afterward receive me to glory." "The wicked shall be turned into hell, and all the nations that forget God:" Ps. ix. "Then shall the righteous shine forth as the sun in the kingdom of their Father:" Matt. xiii. 43. Thus, the idea that a just God governs the universe, involves the necessity of a future judgment; and a future judgment of man involves the necessity of a resurrection, in order that the human persons—not the souls—not the bodies, but the entire persons, soul and body united, may pass before the Judge and receive a just sentence. Hence "there shall be a resurrection of the dead, both of the just and unjust:" Acts xxiv. 15. Objections to this doctrine, based on the difficulties about identity, the reader of Chapter XXII. will, we hope, find no difficulty in refuting; and especially if he turn to 1 Cor. xv. and read Paul's refutation, deduced from the analogies of nature.

In this work, the Spirit of God, who is the great power of Christ, breathes into the body spiritual that mysterious life which is proper to its nature: and as to the redeemed, of whose resurrection only the apostle treats, it is a movement in sanctification. Then follows the judgment. "Because he hath appointed a day, in which he will judge the world in righteousness, by that man whom he hath ordained: whereof he hath given assurance unto all men, in that he hath raised him from the dead." Acts xvii. 31. This judgment, like all other just judgments, is simply declaratory. It does not *make* the wicked, wicked; or the righteous, righteous. It simply *declares* the pre-existent facts of the actual moral character and legal relations of the parties judged; the evidence thereof in the previously developed holy or unholy lives of the parties; and the inevitable legal consequences:— "Some to everlasting life; and some to shame and everlasting contempt:" Dan. xii. 2. "And these shall go away into everlasting punishment: but the righteous into life eternal:" Matt. xxv. 46. The same word, in the original, is used to define the duration of the punishment and of the life: and this dread sentence is a confirmation, equally and alike, of the two classes respectively; the one in a state of misery inconceivable; the other in a state of happiness incomprehensible. No change of character and condition can ever take place. Change, indeed, in degree of happiness or misery, there may be—there must be: but change in condition, never.

For we must farther remark, that confirmation, whilst it is an end of probation, is not an end of moral government. As before stated, we cannot even conceive of an intelligent moral agent existing outside of moral government—not accountable for his actions to the God of the universe. "Why dost thou strive against him? for he giveth no account of his matters:" Job xxxiii. 13. The Creator is the only irresponsible intelligence in the universe which he made. All are accountable, and for ever must and will be, to the universal Governor. Consequently, neither of these classes that pass away from the judgment-seat of Jesus Christ, pass away from under the Divine government. Both, on the contrary, continue subjects of his almighty administration. Therefore he says, "Come, ye blessed of my Father, inherit the kingdom prepared for you," &c. They continue in his kingdom, and subject to his government for ever. The righteous are now officially recognized as citizens of the everlasting kingdom. They can go no more out, for they are "pillars in the temple of my God." The Divine power and faithfulness are for ever pledged to keep them in the love of God and the love of God in them. Indeed, the idea, that Jesus is a confirming head of moral influences to the angelic hosts, that have ever shown such alacrity in his service; and also to the entire universe of virtuous intelligences, is so grand, and glorious, and magnificent, that my heart bounds with joy at its conception, whilst my understanding adoringly refuses to raise a doubt by way of objection. But to illustrate and defend a thought which throws such a halo of glory around the manger, Gethsemane, and the cross, in the closing chapter of a work so small as this, is utterly impracticable, and must, at least for the present, be waived; that we may attend for a moment to some consequences of the saints' confirmation in the everlasting kingdom.

1. Peccability—liability to fall into sin is no part of virtue. The opposite has been affirmed. Dr. Priestley and others who deny the divinity of Christ, and affirm him to be, or to have been, a mere man, have also added, *fallible :* Christ was a *fallible* man. And these *fallible* men argue, that, whilst he never did fall into sin; yet he must have been liable thereto, or he could not be virtuous: thus making

sin, not only *incidental* to any moral system, as does the New Haven divinity; but liability to sin —peccability, an essential requisite in the character of Him who saves his people from their sins.

2. The saints in glory, after the judgment, being still members of the kingdom of God and, by reason of their confirmation in bliss, incapable of any but holy actions, must move onward toward perfection, in a vastly increased ratio. All that has just been said of the souls after death in this regard, is equally, yea, more abundantly, true of the entire sanctified humanity: and thus again, we see how and why the life beyond the judgment must be an everlasting progress in holiness. The holiness and the happiness are eternal parallels.

Let it not be objected, that the saints will become as holy and as happy as God himself. We will admit the inference as legitimate, *if* only you will prove that God is finite in holiness and in happiness. But as he is infinite, no number of finite steps toward him can constitute an approximation, much less an arrival.

Nor yet, let the suggestion be entertained that the saints in glory are never perfectly happy: for the semblance of difficulty here depends simply upon the vagueness of the term *perfect*. Here are two vessels, one a pint measure, the other a gallon. Now pour water into both until it overflows. Are they not both *perfectly* full? And yet how different the bulk and amount? So the saints in glory differ in advancement and capacity; but the capacity of each and every one is full to overflowing. They are all perfectly blessed.

One more aspect of the law of progress, it may be profitable to notice: although it is not strictly within our grand topic of sanctification. It is the fearful question, does the law of progress rule in the world of woe? Do those who "go away into everlasting fire, prepared for the devil and his angels"—into "the lake that burneth with fire and brimstone: which is the second death:" Rev. xxi. 8—do they grow in wickedness and power to resist God? Is the pit of destruction properly called, the abyss, "the bottomless pit?" Rev. xx. 2, 3. "Tophet is ordained of old, yea for the king it is prepared; he hath it deep and large: the pile thereof is fire and much wood; the breath of the Lord, like a stream of brimstone, doth kindle it:" Isa. xxx. 33. Is there anything in the analogies of the two cases, that shuts us up to the terrible conviction, that hell is without a bottom as well as without an end? With trembling heart let us utter a few remarks.

1. The torments of the wicked—the finally impenitent and unbelieving, who despise the overtures of God's mercy and grace, who "trample under foot the Son of God and put him to an open shame, and do despite unto the Spirit of grace"—the torments of the wicked are without end. The self-same word used by the Judge upon his great white throne,

to describe the duration of heaven, is also used to describe the duration of the fire that is never quenched. Other terms equally explicit might be adduced, but we forbear.

2. The wicked, as we have seen, are still subjects of the Divine government, and must for ever remain so. Unless we are prepared for the blasphemous doctrine, that they have sinned themselves out from and beyond God's power, we must believe them accountable for all their actions. But now all their acts are sinful, and therefore must be punished.

3. There is nothing in punishment to generate love toward the law and the governor that executes punishment: but directly the reverse. Hatred of God, therefore, and of his law necessarily result from the endurance of penal evil. Therefore,

4. Purgatory—a place of punishment, where, by painful endurance, the wretched sinner is cleansed like a fœtid clay pipe, from his pollution, and his heart prepared for the exercise of love and holiness, is about the most unphilosophical conceit the devil ever invented to delude lost men. The blood of Calvary is unavailing; the strivings of the Holy Ghost are resisted successfully; the cries and tears, and entreaties of his friends, and the whole church— all fall upon the heart of stone without melting it into contrition, penitence, and love. Now send him to purgatory. Let the devil try him—he'll soon change him. Soon the wicked wretch will be con-

verted, his heart melted into love, and he become fit for an habitation in glory. The blasphemy is as horrible as the philosophy is absurd. Oh sinner, trust not to purgatory, but to the blood of Christ.

5. The just punishment (as in remark 2) occasions (not causes) an increase in wicked actions; this increased activity in sin calls for additional punishment; and thus onward without end. It is a fearful fire that feeds itself: and thus is ensured an eternity of torment, because here is an eternity of sinning. The wretched inhabitant of the burning lake buffets its billows with sinewy arms, and blasphemes the God of justice. Then comes a thunderbolt of Divine wrath, justly due for his recent sin, and sinks him deeper into the fiery flood. Again, rising in increased fury, he belches out the fiery liquid, mixed with still more horrid curses and blasphemy against God, whose justice and holiness again thunder him down to a more profound depth: and thus the worm never dies—the fire is never quenched.

> "Sad world indeed; ah! who can bear
> For ever there to dwell?
> For ever sinking in despair,
> In all the pains of hell?"

And now, dear readers, we must part. At the intersection of two planes we stand. Along one or the other we must move; there is not a third. One ascends beyond the moon, and sun, and planets, and milky way, and all the stars of God; and loses itself in the cloudless effulgence of the Sun of righteousness—that Sun which set in blood on Calvary, but burst the darkness and bondage of the grave and arose to the zenith of his glory and power; and now illumines and controls the destinies of the universe. The other plane descends, cutting the regions of darkness and old night, where no ray from the glorious Sun ever enters; no harp to praise redeeming love ever quivers in the exulting soul—hope dies, and long despair reigns in eternal silence there.

On which of these do you stand? Along which are you moving? I say *moving*, for stationary you cannot be. Ah! do you hesitate? Are you in doubt? Oh! why delay an hour? no time should be lost. "Behold I stand at the door and knock; if any man hear my voice, and open the door, I will come in to him and will sup with him, and he with me:" Rev. iii. 20. And for your farther encouragement, there stands, Luke xi. 13, the heart-cheering promise, and the resistless argument, "If ye then, being evil, know how to give good gifts unto your children: how much more shall your heavenly Father give the Holy Spirit to them that ask him?"

INDEX.

A.
	PAGE
Ability, Three Kinds	28
Afflictions, Means of Sanctification	121

B.
	PAGE
Baptism, A Means of Sanctification	123
Bates,—Quotation from	50
Beatific Vision	23
Believing, Distinguished from Faith	103
Blessed, Two Words so Translated—Explained	22
Butler, Bp., Quotation from	144

C.
Confirmation, not an End of Moral Agency	159
Conscience, Terrors of, not Desirable	42
Improvable	111
Contents	4
Conviction of Sin	38
Not of itself a Blessing	40
Not Conversion, Danger of mistake	41

D.
Death, Negative Sanctification completed at	141
Doubting on account of Indwelling Sin	140
Dreams about Spiritual Things	74

E.
Emotions or Feelings distinguished from Conviction of Sin	74 76
Evidences of Regeneration	70

F.
Faculty, New, Restored in Regeneration	68

F.
Faith, A Duty and a Grace	84 89
Distinguished from Believing	103

G.
Graces, Order of	102

H.
Happiness	14
Right Action Necessary to	15 21
Perfection of	161
Indefinitely Increases	162
Holiness	10
Twofold, Negative, and Positive	11
Holy Life, Proof of Regeneration	97
Holy Spirit, the Sanctifier	44 77

I.
Inability, Moral, a Sin	29
No Excuse for Sin	30
Indwelling of the Holy Ghost	80
Intellect improvable	110

J.
Judgment—A confirmation in Bliss and in Misery	156
Justification and Sanctification compared	98

K.
Knowledge, its Increase strengthens Conscience	112

L.
Life	106 107
Of Spirit	109 115
Love of Life Universal and Necessary to Moral Accountability	18
To God, Evidence of Regeneration	76 104

INDEX.

M.
	PAGE
Memory necessary to Identity	147
Mysteriousness of Regeneration	67

N.
Necessity, Absolute or Conditional	59

P.
Perfection in Sanctification, Negative at death; Positive in Eternity	139
Perseverance in Grace a Necessity	154
In Sin ensures Torments to be Eternal	156
Prayer	129
Preface	8
Progress of Sanctification, Indefinite	106
Providences, Means of Sanctification, War, Sickness, &c	34

R.
Regeneration, Holiness begun	47 49

| PAGE
Regeneration, its Nature, Instantaneousness ... 55
Soul Passive in ... 56 103
Resurrection ... 156

S.
Sanctification, term defined	10
A Work—Instrumentalities	32
Self-love	19
Spirit, Holy, alone gives Life	37 59
Ministry of	26

T.
Temptation, Prayer	126
The Truth Progressive	106 115 118

U.
Unpardonable Sin	45 126

W.
Words not Vehicles of Thought	9

www.ingramcontent.com/pod-product-compliance
Lightning Source LLC
Chambersburg PA
CBHW020309170426
43202CB00008B/550